Phonetic Data Analysis

Phonetic
Data Analysis

An Introduction to Fieldwork and Instrumental Techniques

Peter Ladefoged

Blackwell
Publishing

© 2003 by Peter Ladefoged

350 Main Street, Malden, MA 02148-5020, USA
108 Cowley Road, Oxford OX4 1JF, UK
550 Swanston Street, Carlton, Victoria 3053, Australia

First published 2003 by Blackwell Publishing Ltd

Library of Congress Cataloging-in-Publication Data

Ladefoged, Peter.
Phonetic data analysis : an introduction to fieldwork and instrumental
  techniques / Peter Ladefoged.
      p.   cm.
  Includes index.
    ISBN 0-631-23269-9 (hard. : alk. paper) — ISBN 0-631-23270-2
  (pbk. : alk. paper)
    1. Phonetics—Fieldwork.   2. Phonetics—Methodology.   I. Title.
    P221.L228 2003
  414′.8—dc21

                                                          2003005416

A catalogue record for this title is available from the British Library.

Set in 10/12¹/₂pt Palatino, Palatino PDA book, Palatino Phonetic New
by Graphicraft Limited, Hong Kong
Printed and bound in the United Kingdom
by T.J. International, Padstow, Cornwall

For further information on
Blackwell Publishing, visit our website:
http://www.blackwellpublishing.com

Contents

Preface

If you want to describe how people talk, you have to record some data and then analyze it. This is true whether you are investigating the variant pronunciations of street names in Los Angeles for a speech recognition company, or working as a missionary translating the Bible into a little-known tongue. The basic techniques are the same irrespective of whether you are going into the wilds of the Brazilian rain forest to record the sounds of Banawa, or into the streets of a big city to find out how the homeboys talk. Even obtaining data from a carefully controlled group in a laboratory experiment is really a kind of fieldwork. You need to determine how to set up an appropriate group and how to elicit the speech sounds you are trying to investigate.

This book has two main aims. The first is to consider the fieldwork required for making a description of the sounds of a language. The second is to illustrate the basic techniques of experimental phonetics, most of them requiring little more than a tape recorder, a video camera, and a few other items, none of them very expensive, together with a computer and appropriate programs. Thus I have two principal sets of readers in mind: those who are interested in fieldwork techniques, and those who want a simple introduction to the basic tools of instrumental phonetics. I hope this book will be useful in the many universities that do not have phonetics as a major specialty, as well as in fieldwork situations where one can't have a lot of complicated equipment. All investigations of speech, whether in a lab or a classroom, or a distant country, involve an observer and someone whose speech is being observed; and all fieldworkers should be able to return to base with something more than their fieldwork notebooks.

The fieldwork part of the book is based on more than 40 years' experience of studying the sounds of languages, often in fairly remote locations where I could use only such instrumentation as I could carry with me. When in the field I usually worked with another linguist who was familiar with the language and locale, so my fieldwork is not that of the linguist who works extensively on one language. Others are better qualified than me to explain how to live in a small community and study a language as a whole. This book is not an introduction to general fieldwork techniques for linguists. It is an introduction to the techniques for describing the major phonetic characteristics of a language, irrespective of whether it is a little-known endangered language or a major language spoken by millions of people.

The instrumental phonetic problems considered in this book are largely those that one first encounters when making a description of the phonetic properties of a language. The aim is to enable readers to work with a speaker in class, or to go out into the field and make their own discoveries about how the sounds of a language are made. The book provides full descriptions of the techniques that are readily available and do not require the resources of a major phonetics laboratory.

I have assumed a knowledge of how speech sounds are produced, and an understanding of basic phonetic terminology, but little if any knowledge of instrumental phonetics or how to record speakers in the field. I also assume that you have access to a computer, and a speech analysis system. I've written this book using SciconRD's family of analysis programs. They are probably the best set of programs for general speech analysis available, being straightforward and easy to use, but very powerful. If you are using some other system, such as Computer Speech Lab (CSL), Praat or SIL software, you will find you can use similar techniques.

An additional thread running through the book is a series of boxed comments on different aspects of my own fieldwork. They are written in a more anecdotal fashion and can be neglected by those who want to maintain a serious attitude to work in phonetics. They are there for the readers who would like to learn about instrumental phonetics and fieldwork, and want some information on the human aspects of the work. Whether these asides are noted or not, by the end of the book any reader should be able to go out into the Amazonian rain forest and gather data to characterize the sounds of a little-known language, or into the streets of a big city and describe how the locals talk. Whether working in the Kalahari Desert with !Xóõ Bushmen or observing the curious dialect of the neighbors, the basic procedures are the same.

May your fieldwork and analyses go well.

Peter Ladefoged

Acknowledgments

Fieldwork is like heart surgery: you can learn to do it well only by practicing on someone. My great thanks to all those language consultants and subjects in experiments who helped me learn the techniques discussed in this book. I am also grateful to all the linguists, several of whom are mentioned in the text, who took me on trips to meet their consultants and who exposed the glories of their languages to me. Many people have read drafts of this book and have offered comments, permission to use illustrations, and useful suggestions, notably Victoria Anderson, Heriberto Avelino, Barbara Blankenship, Sun-Ah Jun, Pat Keating, Pam Munro, Rebecca Scarborough, Mark Tatham, Henry Teherani, Tony Traill, and Richard Wright. As always, Jenny Ladefoged has been a constant source of encouragement, advice, criticism, faint praise and elegant phrasing.

I often say that when you can measure what you are speaking about, and express it in numbers, you know something about it; but when you cannot measure it, when you cannot express it in numbers, your knowledge is of a meagre and unsatisfactory kind; it may be the beginning of knowledge, but you have scarcely in your thoughts advanced to the state of Science, *whatever the matter may be.*

Sir William Thomson
(later Lord Kelvin)

Numbers are a scientist's security blanket.

Jenny Ladefoged
(formerly Jennifer Macdonald)

1

Recording the Sounds of a Language

1.1 Deciding What to Record

We'll start with the overall aim of describing the major phonetic structures of a language – where the consonants are made, what kinds of
articulation are involved, how the vowels differ in quality and length,
how the pitch varies in different phrases, and other straightforward
phonetic properties. What do you need to know before you can describe
any of these characteristics? The first point, I would suggest, is how
the sounds are organized. Every language has a certain number of
contrasting sounds that can change the meanings of words. Discerning
what sounds contrast, and how they can be combined to form words,
is a major part of phonology. Without knowing the phonology of a
language you cannot describe the phonetics. You need to know what
it is that you have to describe.

Of course, without some knowledge of the sounds, you cannot
describe the phonology of a language. It is a chicken and egg problem.
The phonology has to be clear before you can make a meaningful
description of the phonetics; and without a description of the sounds,
you cannot get very far with the phonology. The two kinds of investigation have to advance hand in hand. Usually when you start working on the phonetic structures of a language, you will be able to find
some previous work that will be helpful. Ideally much of the phonology
will have been worked out already. In this book we will assume that
there has been some prior work on the languages that we are going to
describe. We will take it that at least the sounds that contrast in words
– the phonemes – have been described to some extent. But, as we will

My first fieldwork trip was not a very happy experience. I was a graduate student at Edinburgh University and my supervisor, David Abercrombie, suggested that I should go to the Outer Hebrides (the chain of islands off the north-west coast of Scotland) and learn something about the sounds of Gaelic. I had no idea what to do, and came back after a few days without achieving anything. I had to hide in my room for a week, because I did not want Professor Abercrombie to know that I had come back early. I hope this book will help you do better.

note later, you should never fully trust anyone else's description of the sounds of the language you are investigating. They may have been describing a different dialect, or the language might have changed since their account of it. Or they might have been wrong.

We'll consider first how to investigate the consonants. If we had all the time in the world, we might make a list of words illustrating every consonant before and after every vowel. In most languages, however, consonants have similar characteristics before most vowels, differing only before high vowels when they may become affricated. Given the practical limitations within which we all have to work, a good starting point is a list that illustrates each consonant before two vowels that are very distinct from one another, such as **i** and **a** if they occur in the language. If the language allows syllable-final consonants, then they should also be illustrated after two different vowels. Syllable-final consonants are often very different from syllable-initial consonants. For example both the consonants in the English word *leek* are very different from their counterparts in *keel*. Initial **k** is aspirated, whereas final **k** may be unreleased and preceded by a glottal stop in my English. Initial **l** in this context is slightly palatalized, whereas final **l** is velarized. All such variations should be illustrated in a complete account of the sounds of a language. A minimal word list for English might include *pie, tie, kye, . . . seep, seat, seek, . . . type, tight, tyke, . . .* , and so on. But, given enough time, it should also include consonants with many other vowels.

How do you go about finding all these words? The obvious place to start is with a dictionary of the language, if there is one. You will need to begin by studying the spelling system and working out which sounds correspond to which letters. If you were going to be recording English, for example, you would need to note that words illustrating initial **k** could be found under both 'c' and 'k', and that words illustrating both

My second fieldwork trip was much more enjoyable. By then I was married to Jenny, who had none of my fears about walking up to a stranger's door and asking to record his vowels. We were working for the Linguistic Survey of Scotland, and had been thoroughly prepared by Ian Catford. He told us how to find speakers, and provided us with word lists that he wanted recorded. The weather was sunny, and the rivers teeming with salmon swimming up to spawn. Fieldwork provides opportunities for seeing many wonderful sights. On later occasions we've seen thousands of pink flamingos rising from a lake, and Everest wreathed in clouds.

θ and ð could be found by looking for the spelling 'th'. Go through the whole dictionary carefully, noting how many pages are given to each consonant in initial position, and then, while looking more closely at a couple of the more common consonants, find out how many columns are devoted to each vowel. By using the most common consonants and vowels you can usually find good sets of minimally contrasting words.

What do you do if no dictionary is available? The prior work on the language may not include a dictionary. It may be just a few notes by a linguist and perhaps a folk tale or short illustrative sample. Even this can provide a useful start. Type the story and any other words available into a computer and then sort them alphabetically. (Replace all spaces between words by paragraph marks, and then get the computer to sort the list.) Even a short word list like this can be useful in finding words. It will give you an indication of which are the most frequent sounds, and where you will find it easiest to find sets of minimal contrasts.

When you are looking around for sets of words, another major source is the speakers of the language themselves. Your short word list may have led you to find a set that almost illustrates the sounds you are interested in, but it lacks a particular example. Make up a word that might be appropriate, and ask the speakers if it exists. You may find that is the name of one of their clans, or a particular kind of tree, or some other perfectly acceptable but less frequently used word. Find out if your speakers can rhyme words or use alliteration in any way. This may help them produce good contrasting sets. If you are working on a well-known language, you might be able to find a rhyming dictionary (there are several for English), giving you a direct lead on minimal sets such as *pea, tea, key,* . . . .

Generally speaking, it is best to avoid nonsense words, particularly if you are going to be dealing with naive speakers. Many people find it difficult to pronounce a nonsense word in a natural way. So should my list for English have included *kye*, a perfectly good word that has dropped out of use and is not in the vocabulary of most speakers of English? Usually literate speakers can pronounce simple forms such as this without any difficulty, particularly if you explain that *kye* is an older variant of the plural of *cow*. In any circumstances, you should always stick to words that speakers feel comfortable with. You might have to remind them that the word in question is what hunters call a particular type of arrow, or a bird that is rarely seen nowadays. But in the end, all that matters is that you have a list of words that speakers can pronounce in a natural way, with the true sounds of their own language.

It is very important to have a set of words that are as near minimal contrasts as possible, even if it means including a few unusual words. When it comes to characterizing the difference between sounds, the surrounding sounds should be identical. For example, as we will see in chapter 5, when you describe the vowels of a language you will find differences in the qualities of a set of vowels after **p** in comparison with those after **t**. A single list with some vowels after the one consonant and others after the other would lead to a false description of the differences in vowel quality. In most languages vowels differ even more before different syllable-final consonants. To take the example we looked at before, consider the vowels in *keel* and *leek*. Because of the final **l**, the vowel in *keel* is usually much more diphthongal than that in *leek*.

It is usually impossible to get a complete list illustrating all the consonants before the same vowel. Some consonants may occur only at the ends of words, or only after certain vowels. There is, for example, no set of words illustrating all the fricatives of English in the same circumstances, largely because English originally had no contrasts between voiced and voiceless fricatives, and the sound **ʒ**, a very recent import, occurs at the beginnings of only a few foreign words such as *Zsa Zsa* and at the ends of loan words such as *rouge*. You just have to find the best set you can, using a number of different possibilities. You might start with *fie, vie, thigh, thy, sigh, Zion, shy*, which contains all the fricatives in initial position before **aɪ** except for **ʒ**. Another set such as *proof, prove, sooth, soothe, loose, lose, rouge* contains all the fricatives in final position after **uː** except **ʃ**. Then you could add one of the few contrasts between ʃ and **ʒ**, *Aleutian* vs. *allusion*. Not very satisfactory, but there is no perfect answer for this set of sounds.

Linguists refer to a pair of words that contrast in only one segment as a minimal pair. A set of words that is the same except for a single segment is a minimal set. In Hawaiian, for example, it is easy to find a minimal set contrasting all the consonants (there are only 8 of them, **p, k, ʔ, m, n, w, l, h**). It took me only a few minutes using a Hawaiian dictionary to find: **paka, kaka, ʔaka, maka, naka, waka, laka, haka**, meaning *to remove the dregs, to rinse* or *clean, to laugh, eye, to quiver* or *shake, sharp* or *protruding, tame* or *gentle, shelf* or *perch*. With a set of words like this, we can compare the properties of each consonant with those of the others, knowing that they are not being affected by the context. If Hawaiian had not had the word **paka** (or you and your consultant had not been able to find it), you might have used the word **pika**. But then, when you compared the duration of the aspiration in **p** and **k** (a topic we will discuss more fully in chapter 4), you would have found that **p** had more aspiration than **k**. But, other things being equal (i.e. when they are in minimally contrasting words), it is the other way around; Hawaiian **k** has slightly more aspiration than **p**, as it does in most languages of the world. It is just that before **i** all stops generally have more aspiration. The initial **k** in the Hawaiian word **kika** has even more than in **kaka**.

Dictionaries often illustrate the sounds of a language (meaning the phonemes) simply as they appear in common words, rather than in words that are minimally contrasting. Similarly linguists who are not concerned with phonetics sometimes list the phonemes in words that are far from minimal sets. If the primary aim is to describe the syntax of a language, then there is little need to know more than that the sounds all differ from one another. But from a phonetic point of view it is well worth taking an enormous amount of trouble to find the best possible minimally contrasting sets of words.

You should also check that you have all the possible sounds. As I mentioned earlier, the source that you are using as a basis for making a word list may not be fully accurate. Your speakers will tell you if they no longer have a certain sound, or consider it to belong to another dialect, but they may not think of pointing out additional sounds. Look at the consonant inventory and see if there are any obvious gaps. For example, the language may have **p, t, k** and the ejectives **t', k'**. Ask if there are any words beginning with **p'**. There may not be, as many languages have **t', k'** but lack **p'**, but you should

Always when doing fieldwork you must be sensitive to the culture around you. Some words may be taboo because they are associated with people who have recently died. Others may be parts or functions of the body that are not mentioned in polite company. On some occasions, when looking for a particular sound in a particular context, I've said 'Do you have a word that sounds like such-and-such?', and provoked roars of laughter or embarrassed looks. In a polite book like this, I can't tell you about some of the words I hit on. When an unexpected reaction occurs I just go on with something different.

check for missing possibilities. Similarly, if neighboring languages or languages of the same family have sounds that do not seem to be in the language you are investigating, ask about them, demonstrating them in a variety of simple syllables, and inquiring whether there are any words with those syllables. You may find that your language consultants come up with sounds that are not in your sources.

A language will have a certain set of phonemes that form the contrasts between words. Each of these phonemes will have a number of allophones – members of a phoneme that occur in specific contexts. The word list should illustrate the principal allophones of consonants. If it already contains syllable-initial and syllable-final consonants, many allophonic differences will have been included, but there may be other interesting allophones that should be noted. A word list for American English, for example, should illustrate what happens to t in *pity* (where it is a tap) and in *button* (where it is often accompanied or replaced by a glottal stop). A really detailed study of English would include all the consonant clusters that can occur. But as there are approximately 105 ways of beginning an English syllable, and about 143 ways of ending one (depending on what you count as a cluster), this would be excessive for most purposes.

Illustrating vowels follows along the same lines. Make a list that has all the vowels in as similar contexts as possible. Sometimes that's easy. Japanese has several sets such as **ki, ke, ka, ko, ku**, all of which are meaningful words. In other languages it may be more difficult. You can very nearly get a complete set of English vowels in monosyllables beginning with **b** and ending with **d** or **t**, but to be complete you have to include another set beginning with **h** and ending with **d**, so as to get the vowel in *hood*. In any case, include sets of vowels after different consonants. If you take the Japanese set **ki, ke, ka, ko, ku** you will find that the vowels may be a little different (they are usually slightly higher) than they are in Japanese **mi, me, ma, mo, mu** (but in this set they may be slightly nasalized).

Vowels often have important allophones that should be illustrated. In English, for example, the set of vowels that can occur before **ŋ** is restricted. There are different vowels in *seen* and *sin*, but before **ŋ** in *sing* there is no such contrast. In Californian English the vowel in *sing* is closer to that in *seen*, but in most forms of British English it is closer to that in *sin*. Special lists are needed to illustrate these context-restricted systems. Consonants often have a noticeable effect on vowel quality. Vowels before final **l** and **r** are very different from those before final **d** in English, and (to use more distant fieldwork examples) vowels adjacent to the uvulars **q, χ** are lower in Aleut.

Many languages contrast oral and nasal vowels. In some languages vowel length is important. These contrasts have to be illustrated, along with any other contrasts such as those involving different voice qualities, a topic that we will discuss more fully in a later chapter.

It is often a good idea to record words within a carrier sentence, a frame that surrounds the contrast being illustrated. There are two reasons for this. Firstly, whenever anyone says a list of words, there is a tendency to produce them with the special intonation pattern used for lists. If you ask a speaker of English to say a list of words such as *heed, hid, head, had,* the last word will almost invariably be produced with a lower pitch and a longer vowel than it would have had if it had been earlier in the sequence. One can avoid this by adding some unneeded words at the end, making the list, for instance, *heed, hid, head, had, hid, heed.* But a better technique for producing stability in the pronunciation of each word is to put it into a frame such as *Say ____ again.* Even when eliciting lists in this way, it is a good idea to have the first item repeated again; otherwise the whole frame sentence may occur on a lower pitch, as sometimes happens for the last sentence in a paragraph when reading English.

The second reason for using a frame around the illustrative words is that it makes it easier to measure the lengths of the items that contrast. With a frame such as *Say ____ again* one can determine the beginnings and ends of stop consonants, which would be impossible if there were other stops or silence before and after them. It may be necessary to use more than one frame. If you want to measure the length of a word containing only vowels (such as, the words *eye, owe, awe* in English) you couldn't do it if it were in the frame *Say ____ again*, as there would be no separation between the words. The vowels of the words in the frame would run into the vowels of the test words. You would do better with a frame like *Repeat ____ twice*, which lets you see words beginning or ending with vowels.

Whatever language you are working on, while doing the preliminary work of determining a word list you also need to find suitable frames. In French I have used *Dis ___ encore*, the equivalent of *Say ____ again* both in meaning and in enclosing the test word between vowels. In Korean I used **ikəsi ____**, 'This is ___'. Even a simple frame helps speakers get into a set way of talking when recording, so that they say each word in the same manner. A frame ensures that each word occurs in the same rhythmic position, which is important as the position in an utterance can affect the stress pattern and length. It is usually best to begin by recording words in a frame that ensures that they have the equivalent of the nuclear stress in a sentence.

Finally, there must be material that illustrates the suprasegmental aspects of the language – variations in stress, tone and intonation. (Length distinctions have been mentioned already.) In a tone language, the word list must include words that illustrate the contrasting tones, each on at least two different vowels. If stress is significant, as it is in English, the list must include forms such as *an insult, to insult, to differ, to defer*. Speakers sometimes find such contrasts difficult to make when they are not in meaningful sentences. It may be necessary to use special frames that are not absolutely identical, using comparable sentences such as *Lance insults our Dad* vs. *Len's insults are bad*.

Intonation patterns are often hard to illustrate, as the phonological contrasts in many languages have not been systematized. But it is worth recording sentences illustrating commands, statements and

---

Once, when I was recording with a colleague in Africa, we had a speaker who wanted to tell us traditional stories. He was a good story teller, with lots of rhetorical flourishes that gave rise to the formulaic responses of the people around ('Say it again, father', 'So be it, so be it'). The first story he told us was a great performance, and my colleague wanted to record him telling some more. But we had very little knowledge of the language and would not be able to make a translation. We were never going to be able to use any of it for any scientific analysis. It was a great performance, but we asked him to stop so we could get on with our work.

different types of questions, and other syntactic devices that are conveyed by intonation changes, as well as differences in focus, such as *I want a* **red** *pen not a black one,* as compared with *I want a red* **pen** *not a pencil.*

So far I have been suggesting a very structured way of getting data that will illustrate the sounds of a language. The principal data will be word lists for the phonemic contrasts and specific sentences for describing the basic intonational patterns. It is also a good practice to record some more conversational utterances. I usually ask speakers to tell me about something simple, such as what they did yesterday. I try to elicit three or four sentences, not more, and then get the speaker, or someone working with me, to translate each sentence into English. There's not much that can be done with recordings that lack written translations and good phonetic transcriptions (which I try to do the same evening or as soon as I can). From a phonetician's point of view there is no point in making lengthy recordings of folk tales, or songs that people want to sing. Such recordings can seldom be used for an analysis of the major phonetic characteristics of a language, except in a qualitative way. You need sounds that have all been produced in the same way so that their features can be compared. From the point of view of a fieldworker wanting long-term ties to the community, it is worthwhile spending time establishing rapport with speakers. But at times you may have to tactfully remind your consultants that, as we will discuss in the next section, work on their language is work and not play.

When you have a tentative list of words and phrases that you want to record, it is time to start working with one or two speakers of the language. Even if you know almost nothing about the language, and there are no books or articles on it or any closely related language, it is

One of the best lists of words that I was able to record illustrates the 20 clicks of Nama, a Khoisan language spoken in Namibia. I was working with an excellent consultant, Mr. Johannes Boois of the Namibian Literacy Bureau. After a little while he said, 'Oh I see what you are trying to do, you want a set of words, each with one of the Nama clicks at the beginning, and each before the same vowel. Let me think about it.' Next morning he came back with a list of words of just that kind. He added, 'You didn't say whether you wanted them all on the same tone, but I found words that all had high tone vowels.'

advisable to make some sort of list before contacting anyone. Your list will give the speakers some indication of what you are trying to do, and working together you will be able to develop a better list.

You will need to go through your list very carefully with your selected speakers. (We'll see in the next section how to find appropriate language consultants.) Usually a number of problems arise the first time through. Some of the words will turn out to be used only by old people, or women, or speakers of another dialect. If you are lucky your language consultants will grasp what you are trying to do, and suggest alternative words. Get them talking among themselves, and they may even be able to suggest contrasts that you had not anticipated. Pay attention to what they have to say, and try to imitate their pronunciation. When you have learned to say a word yourself in a way that a native speaker will accept, you will have found out a great deal about how it is articulated. Moreover it is very satisfying to your language consultants to hear your attempts at speaking their language. One of the first things you should do when working with someone is to learn how to say 'hello' and 'goodbye'. If you greet people properly, showing respect for their language, they will be much more relaxed and willing to help you find a set of illustrative words. You should also be able to say 'please' and 'thank you' to people in their own language (make your mother proud of how you behave).

There is no special trick involved in imitating the pronunciation of a word. It's not like being able to imitate someone's voice or impersonate a particular character, skills I've never had. Repeating a single word that you have just heard is simply a matter of learning to listen for subtle shades of sounds, and learning to produce them. In my experience most students can produce nearly all the sounds on the IPA chart fairly well after a ten-week course in phonetics, provided that they have an instructor leading them through a set of practical exercises such as those in my textbook *A Course in Phonetics* (Heinle & Heinle, 2001). Becoming fully proficient in producing and hearing some complex sounds may take a little longer. I'm still unable to produce a voiced palatal click in a way that fully satisfies a speaker of !Xóõ. But given a proper basic training in phonetics, with a little practice anyone can achieve a near-native pronunciation of most short words. Phonetic ability is not an esoteric skill possessed by only a few.

When you are checking that you have pronounced a word correctly, be careful how you phrase your question. If you just ask 'Am I saying this correctly?', some language consultants will approve your mispronunciation simply because they want to make you feel good. Tell them that you want them to be very strict teachers, and that you want to sound exactly like them. You should also be aware that when a consultant doesn't like your pronunciation of a word it may not be for the reason you expect. You may be trying to get the correct pronunciation of the consonant cluster at the beginning of a word and find that you are continually told that you are saying the word wrong. But it may not be the consonant cluster that is wrong; you may have got the wrong tone on the vowel, or something else quite different.

A technique that I find better than simply saying a word and asking 'Am I saying this correctly?', is to produce two slightly different versions, and ask 'Which is better, one or two?' I usually repeat a pair of possibilities several times, holding up one finger when I say the first possibility and two fingers when I say the second. If neither is approved it may well be that I am working on altering the wrong part of the word. When approval has been given to one of the two possibilities, I go on with something else and later return to the same pair, but saying them in reverse order, to see if they still prefer the same one. With good consultants you can even take a word one syllable at a time, checking several possibilities for each syllable.

I cannot emphasize too much the importance of working with speakers and thinking out what it is that has to be illustrated before making formal sets of recordings. The word list will no doubt be revised several times during later work with additional speakers, but almost nothing in the study of the phonetic characteristics of a language is more important than this initial work on a word list. You should be prepared to spend many hours checking everything out. You have to be sure that you record all that you will want to analyze. When you have left the field you will no longer have access to a large group of speakers.

Finally in this section, I should note that the formal recordings that I have suggested making are only the first step in describing the phonetic events that occur in a language. In normal conversation we don't use the precise pronunciations that are used when repeating lists of words. A full description of a language will try to account for all the elided forms and the vagaries of casual speech. Making suitable recordings for this kind of analysis involves catching people when they are bound up with what they are saying and have forgotten that they are being recorded. Such recordings are valuable for many tasks, such as building speech recognition systems. Make them, and, most importantly, annotate them while you can still remember what they are about. But they are not a good basis for a description of the phonetic structures of a language. You need to know the contrastive sounds that occur before you can describe conversational utterances.

1.2   Finding Speakers

Probably the question that I am asked most frequently is: 'How do you find appropriate speakers?' There is no general answer. Local conditions vary greatly. In many parts of the world official permission is required before doing any kind of research, and sometimes this works out to one's advantage. There may be a local official to whom one must report, who may be able to help. Often a local schoolteacher, who may not speak the language you are interested in, nevertheless knows people who do. The local postmaster is another good source of information, as are local clergy and police (though in many societies these authority figures may have been brought in from another region, and not be looked on with favor by the local population).

It may turn out that none of these suggestions is any use when you are trying to work with a very isolated group of people. In these circumstances the only way I have ever been able to achieve anything is to find a linguist or a missionary who has lived in the area and can point out the best consultants to me. They can also help me find an assistant who knows both English and the local trade language that the speakers of the language I am investigating will know. I've done well with the help of schoolboys who translated what I wanted to ask into Swahili, which is the lingua franca of many parts of East Africa. The language consultants I was working with knew Swahili (most speakers of small community languages are multilingual), and could produce the words I wanted in their own language.

Sometimes it is very difficult to work on a particular language. Native American communities may want you to get permission from their tribal council. They may be suspicious of your motives and feel that you may be stealing something from them. The language is sacred for many Native Americans in a way that is hard for outsiders to appreciate. It was given to them by the Gods, and is an essential part of their religion and their identity. In these circumstances one should be very careful not to give offence, and offer to show everything to the

One of our former UCLA linguistics students who is a Navajo tells how she was once giving a talk in a Navajo community. She was showing how words could be put together to create new words (just as *sweet + heart* creates a word with an entirely new meaning). While she was explaining this an elder called out: 'Stop this blasphemy! Only the gods can create words.' The Navajo language is holy in a way that is very foreign to most of us.

tribal council before publishing it in any way. Speakers may also feel they are being exploited and think that fieldworkers are making money out of them (as, indeed, we are, in that we are usually being paid to do fieldwork and are receiving the rewards of the publication of the knowledge we acquired from them). However, although a few Native American communities may be hard to work in, others are welcoming. They are very conscious of the fact that their language is spoken only by people who are middle-aged or older. When their children grow up the language will be gone. As a result they are eager to have linguists do whatever they can so that at least a record of the language exists.

There are various points to watch for when selecting speakers. The first is to make sure that the language is really their mother tongue. This may seem too obvious to mention, but there have been cases of well-known linguists publishing authoritative grammars based on the speech of non-native speakers. You want speakers who use the language in their daily life, have all their teeth, and are not hard of hearing. You should also consult to find out who are considered to be the 'best' speakers, particularly if you are working on an endangered language that people no longer speak fluently. Unfortunately you will often be told that the best speaker is a very elderly person, who may be missing their teeth, and who would rather reminisce than con-centrate on going through a word list. In literate countries you may be directed to a local scholar whose help you should certainly seek, while emphasizing that you want to learn how ordinary people speak. You'll probably get a shrug of the head, and be told that they don't speak properly nowadays. But be insistent and you'll avoid all the spelling pronunciations and hypercorrections you might otherwise get from someone with a vested interest in the language.

It is worth spending time trying to find somebody who is quick and eager to help. If after a short session you find any problems, move on. When you are working on the sounds, people may not realize that you are not interested in the precise meanings of each word. Once you have a meaning that is sufficient to identify the word for other people, you do not need to know that the word also means a particular type of tree, or the left arm of a new-born babe. Old people can be hard to control. Given a choice I like to work with high-school students. They quickly understand what I am trying to do, and like to act as teachers, correcting my attempts to repeat what they are saying.

Many speakers are interested in their language, and willing to work for nothing. But it is a good practice to insist that it *is* work, and they should be paid – if they want to, they can always give the money to charity. I find it much easier if there is a regular professional relationship between the speakers and myself. They are then more willing to provide the data I want and not to digress. Speakers are often reassured about accepting payment if you can point out that it is not your money, but money that has been given to you so that you can do this work. On some occasions a gift to the community might be more appropriate – I once bought a cow for a group of Kalahari Bushmen who were trying to start a herd. Many groups have a cultural center that would welcome support.

A good basis for determining the rate of pay is to offer twice the wage that they might otherwise be earning. If they are not in regular employment, then twice the wage that a laborer in the fields might get seems fair. Paying at a much higher rate is unfair in another way. Other linguists working in the area will not bless you if you have inflated the local economy by paying too much. But you should, of course, always offer to provide something to eat and drink; and, alas, tobacco is often welcome. In communities that would like a linguist's help, I am delighted to offer what services I can, such as providing recordings and annotated word lists. But I don't like it when people expect too much. I've known cases when people think they are offering me something that is worth more than ten times the hourly rate for part-time work by university undergraduates. I won't deal with people like that, and just move on.

Another question that I am often asked is: 'How many speakers do I need to record?' Ideally you want about half a dozen speakers of each sex. There may be systematic differences between male and female speech. In Pirahã, a language spoken in the Amazonian rain forest, women always use /h/ where men have /s/. If you can eventually find 12 or even 20 members of each sex, so much the better. When working on an endangered language, this may not be possible. I've sometimes had to be satisfied with the four or five speakers that I can find. In any case, particularly if you are working on an endangered language, or in a country in which the language is not ordinarily spoken, you should check that each speaker is considered by the others to be a good speaker of the same dialect of the language. Sometimes this requires a certain amount of tact, but you can usually take one of the group aside and ask about the capabilities of the others.

I (and other linguists) used to describe the phonetics of a language on the basis of information from a single speaker. Clearly, a single speaker is no longer enough to satisfy modern standards of phonetic description. Such speakers may not speak in what others consider to be the normal way. They may be more literate, and have their own ideas on how the language 'should' (in their view) be spoken. Groups of ordinary speakers are needed to reflect the true phonetic characteristics of the language.

A final very important point in connection with choosing and working with speakers: before you go into the field consult your institution's Office for the Protection of Research Subjects. In the United States, anyone who is affiliated with any university or other institution that receives federal funds must get permission from their Institutional Review Board (IRB) for any research that involves human subjects. This regulation applies irrespective of where in the world you are working or whether you are also affiliated with an institution in another country. The IRB will want to be assured that your language consultants know all the procedures you are using, and what their rights are. Usually they include being able to withdraw their participation at any time, with no questions asked, and to retain their anonymity, unless they explicitly sign away that right. The IRB will want to know about rates of pay, translation of the agreement that is made with participants, whether minors (such as the high-school students mentioned above) will be involved, how permission for their participation will be obtained, how permission for using photographs of field situations (such as those in this book) will be sought, and many other points.

All good fieldworkers will look after their consultants carefully and not do anything that is harmful in any way. But when out in the field it is sometimes hard to get people to sign a written agreement. Getting signatures, or even a mark on a page, is virtually impossible when dealing with people who have never held a pen or signed a document of any kind in their entire life. When working in the Amazonian rain forest, for example, I've been with people who have had very little contact with the outside world. They are willing to sit and talk for a while, but are reluctant to do anything more. Similarly, in Africa I've met people who are suspicious of formal arrangements. If you are likely to be in these circumstances, you should ask your IRB whether it would be possible to substitute a recording for a written record. You can then make a recording of the procedures being explained to the consultants in their own language or the local trade language. If your consultants show by their comments that they have understood what is going on, and are willing to participate, your IRB may be willing to consider this as informed consent.

Most standard IRB regulations require that the identity of research participants be kept confidential. You should ask your consultants whether they mind their names being revealed. Virtually everybody I've worked with has always been pleased to let it be known that they helped describe their language. It is something that they are proud of doing. You should be sure that your consultants understand they are giving you permission to identify them. Then, in any publication, you can acknowledge them by name. This is a good practice, not only because one should give thanks where thanks are due, but also because it may help other researchers. When in the field, I've often appreciated being able to find consultants that other linguists have worked with.

1.3   Recording Systems

There are many ways of making recordings. A common technique is to use a cassette recorder, but DAT (Digital Audio Tape) and CD recorders are widely available. In addition, systems for recording directly onto a computer offer great advantages. My own preference is to use a portable DAT recorder that is small and inconspicuous. People often get worried when you set up a recording machine or a laptop computer and start checking it out. With a portable DAT recorder you can see that it is working properly before you begin, and walk into a room with it already running in your pocket. Then you simply have to bring out a microphone when it comes to the moment to record. (One could even record without people seeing the microphone, but I always ask permission and let people know they are being recorded. Making surreptitious recordings of anybody anywhere is not normally approved by my (or, probably, any) university's Institutional Review Board.)

Comparing the different systems for making recordings leads to no easy conclusions. There are four properties that one wants from a good recording system, each of which will be considered in turn: (1) a good frequency response (roughly speaking, the range of pitches that the system can record); (2) a good signal/noise ratio (the range of loudness); (3) reliability and user-friendliness; and (4) the possibility of using the recordings for a long time.

The frequency response of a system is a measure of the extent to which it faithfully records and reproduces each frequency. We want pitches that go in at a certain relative loudness to come out at the same relative loudness. We can represent the frequency response of a system by a graph showing the difference in dB (decibels, the unit of intensity, the acoustic correlate of loudness) between the input and the output. The solid horizontal line in figure 1.1 shows a perfect frequency response.

A perfect frequency response is almost what one gets using a DAT recorder or a direct recording onto a computer or CD with a good microphone and Analog to Digital sound system. The thinner solid line in figure 1.1 shows the response of a professional-quality cassette

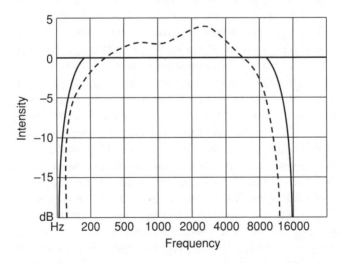

Figure 1.1   The frequency response curves of a perfect recording system (horizontal solid line), a professional cassette recorder (solid curve), and an ordinary cassette recorder (dashed line).

recorder that has been kept in good condition by cleaning the recording and playback heads. It will record within ± 2 dB all the frequencies (roughly the pitches) between 80 Hz (the pitch of a fairly deep bass voice) and 11,000 Hz (almost the highest frequency components in an s). This pitch range is completely satisfactory for nearly all speech projects. The dashed curve is that of a cheaper cassette recorder. It will cut off quite a bit of the bass components in speech, and will also have an uneven response including a severe drop-off in the higher frequencies.

The second factor we have to consider is the background noise in a recording. The amount of noise can be measured by what is called the signal/noise ratio. This is the difference between the signal (the sound you want to record) and the noise (everything else, including both the inherent noise of the system and all the background sounds such as running water, distant TVs, refrigerators, or fans that you want to exclude). The signal/noise ratio is stated in dB. Roughly speaking, when two sounds differ by one dB, there is a just noticeable difference in loudness, and when one sound is twice as loud as another, there is a 5 dB difference. A quiet room often has quite a lot of background noise, making it perhaps 30 dB above the threshold of hearing (the quietest sound that you can just hear). A 40 dB signal/noise ratio will occur if the speech you are trying to record is 80 dB above the threshold of hearing and the background is about 40 dB above that level. CD quality, or sounds recorded directly onto a computer, can have a signal/noise ratio of up to 96 dB, although they seldom get above 84 dB, as there is always noise from the system itself.

Before beginning a recording you should check the signal/noise ratio. You will need to record a short piece first, to see that your recording level is set as high as possible without overloading. Then, when no one is saying anything, if you are recording onto a tape recorder of any kind you should check that the sound level indicator is as low as possible. It is difficult to quantify this on most tape recorders as the recording indicator will not be steady, but it may be hovering around −40 dB. If you are recording directly onto a computer, look at the recording on the screen and run the cursor over it. Most systems will provide a record of the voltage measured in bits. The maximum variation in voltage that you can record will probably be 96 dB, which is equivalent to ± 32,768 bits.

As I sit in my living room, using a computer, but with the microphone unplugged, the system is recording a baseline variation of ± 1 bits, which means that there is 6 dB system noise. With the microphone plugged in but turned off, this increases to ± 2 bits, making the total machine noise 12 dB. With the microphone on but nobody talking, the baseline variation goes up to ± 8 bits with an occasional spike up to ± 32, giving a background noise level of 24 to 36 dB. This still leaves me a 66 dB signal/noise ratio when I record up to the full 96 dB that the system allows. In practice, because I want to stay well below the overload level, I have a usable range on this computer system of 50–60 dB.

Any tape recorder has a range below that, as there is inevitably considerable noise from the tape itself. A professional tape recorder using high-quality tape may have a signal/noise ratio of about 45–50 dB. (I've often heard claims for more, but seldom found them true.) Many cheaper cassette recorders have only a 30 dB range. This is sufficient if you simply want to record the words that are being used, but it is not sufficient for a good acoustic analysis, nor will you be able to use it for a narrow phonetic transcription.

Whether you are using a tape recorder or a computer, it is important to use a high-quality microphone. Built-in microphones, whether on a tape recorder or a computer, are seldom high-quality – they usually cut both the bass and the treble. A condenser microphone, with its own power supply (a small battery, such as those used in watches or hearing aids), will provide the best frequency range. It should have a covering over it, to protect it from the wind and from direct puffs of air from the speaker's mouth. It should also be directional so that it records sound from the front better than from the rear.

The third factor we should consider in comparing recording systems is their reliability and user-friendliness. Cassette recorders are comparatively easy to maintain, but DAT recorders are more complex. When they go wrong, they will probably need to be returned to the manufacturer. Computer and CD recording systems are fairly rugged. User-friendliness from the phonetician's point of view is best summed up by assessing how easy it is to find particular words and to repeat small parts of a recording over and over again, the major listening tasks for phoneticians describing languages. Cassette recorders are fairly easy to use in this way. DAT recorders are more difficult, although they do have the advantage that each section between stops and starts on the original recording is identified by a number, and the time of each event is displayed in real minutes and seconds, rather than by an arbitrary number. Computers win hands down for providing easy

My first paid position in the field of phonetics was as a lab technician, at Edinburgh University. Much of my job consisted of making phonograph records – 78 rpm recordings on vinyl disks. Not many people have the equipment to play these disks now.

finding and repeating of phrases. Selected portions of a waveform can be played repeatedly at the touch of a key without degrading the recording, and a transcription can be put on the screen, directly above the sound wave. Older computer systems were tiresome to use in that one had to stop recording frequently to save files, but this is no longer true, and one can now record reliably for long periods onto gigabyte hard drives.

Finally we must consider how long the recordings are going to last. There are two aspects to this: firstly, how long a particular type of tape or other recording medium will last, and secondly, how long there will be systems on which they can be played. Old-fashioned reel-to-reel tape recordings are still playable after many years, as long as proper precautions have been taken. The main problems that arise are that the tape becomes brittle, and requires careful handling, and there may be some print-through – the transference of the magnetism on one part of the tape to the piece of the tape immediately below it on the reel. The possibility of print-through can be lessened by winding the tape back and then winding it forward before storing it. In 2000 I found that there was only a slight increase in the level of the noise on some reel-to-reel recordings I had made in 1954 (recordings of cardinal vowels by Daniel Jones, now on the web). My only real problem was finding a machine to play them on.

Cassette recordings are probably about as stable as old-fashioned reel-to-reel recordings. They, too, will become brittle over the years. We should also note that every time a tape is copied some noise is added. This is not the case for DAT tapes or CDs, which can be copied with no loss of sound quality. Nobody knows how long DAT recordings will last, or how long they will be popular enough to be supported. Nor do we know the lifetime of CDs if they are properly kept, but we do know that they can be easily scratched and damaged. Computer systems are changing all the time, and it is a good idea to make backup recordings of different kinds to be safe. My best guess is that recording directly onto a computer and making a backup copy on a CD-ROM will, for some time, be the best way of making a high-quality recording and preserving it so that it can be played for many years.

I always try to have a whole backup system for making recordings in the field. You never know when someone is going to spill a mug of water on your machine or a goat will try to eat it. In addition to a DAT recorder and a computer, I travel with a video camera (for reasons that will be discussed in the next chapter), which has excellent sound recording capabilities and can be used as a slightly less convenient backup system when you've unfortunately dropped all your other equipment over the side of the boat.

1.4   Making a Recording

The main problem in making a technically good recording is the elimination of background noise. This is largely a matter of placing the microphone correctly and finding a good, quiet place. The best place for the microphone is as close to the speaker as possible. The place could be a quiet living room (make sure all the doors, especially that to the kitchen, are shut) or somewhere outdoors away from the clamor of the village, with no waterfalls, rustling trees, pounding waves, chickens, chirping cicadas or other animal noises.

Try to keep the level of the recording constant and as high as possible without overloading. In this way the signal (what your speaker is saying) will have a high level relative to the noise (everything else). If you can, it is good to work as a team, with one person ensuring that the proper words are recorded, and the other keeping the level steady while listening for background noise – the refrigerator that has suddenly switched on, or the noisy children drifting closer. It is hard to have to pay attention to the speaker and at the same time look after the recording. As we will see in the next two chapters, field research usually works best when there is somebody watching and controlling the environment leaving someone else to concentrate on the speaker.

I once spoiled an otherwise excellent recording made in the wet season in Nigeria. I was so used to the noise of the rain on the roof that I just didn't realize how loud it was. When I listened to the recording I found I couldn't distinguish some words because of the noise of the rain.

The best way to keep a high signal/noise ratio is to have the speaker as close as possible to the microphone without actually blowing into it. The intensity of a recorded sound depends on the square of the distance between the source of sound and the microphone. Chickens or cars that are 10 m away will not be a problem if the microphone is only 2 cm from the speaker's mouth. Even if they had equal intensities as sources of sounds, at the microphone the speaker would have 250,000 times more intensity than the chickens. You can achieve ratios of this kind and avoid problems due to speakers moving around by using a head-mounted microphone placed just to the side of the lips so as to avoid the direct rush of air in fricatives and stop bursts. If it is also a directional microphone that records sound from the front better than from the rear, the signal/noise ratio will be even better.

There are advantages in recording people one at a time using a head-mounted microphone to control the noise. But there are also advantages to recording people in groups, with one person saying the word or phrase and the rest of the group repeating it. One has to make sure that the leader is a good speaker of the language, so that the others, if they are simply imitating this pronunciation, are at least using a pronunciation that is accepted as being representative of

Recording a group of !Xóõ speakers in the Kalahari Desert. (Photograph by Tony Traill.)

the language. This type of recording takes less time, and has more homogeneity. When I have managed to get a group of people together, I am often unwilling to let them disperse while I record them individually, in case some of them don't come back.

Using a highly directional microphone it is possible to get a good recording by pointing the microphone at the speakers one at a time. This both signals that it is their turn to speak and allows for some adjustment in the intensity of the recording. The microphone can be placed closer to those who speak more softly, and further away from the loud-mouthed types. The disadvantage of this technique is that it involves holding the microphone and moving it – circumstances that are apt to produce unwanted noises. You may be able to place a microphone near the center of a group (preferably so that it is closer to the quieter speakers) and then signal by a hand gesture when it is each person's turn to speak. But in fieldwork situations such control is often not possible.

When recording a group of speakers it is important to make sure that the lead speaker is well respected. It is, for example, inappropriate in most countries to have a young woman as the lead speaker. Whatever your feelings about the status of women, don't try to impose them on a group of young African men, who will only laugh or play the fool when you expect them to take their lead from a young woman. On the other hand, a well-respected older woman is often an excellent choice to lead a group. Sometimes it is easier to get women speakers than men. When working on Montana Salish we had a wonderful group of elderly women, but I had to cajole a number of men into joining us by suggesting that they surely did not want their language to be represented just by women.

In a country in which the speakers are literate, it may be possible to ask speakers to read the list, but this is seldom a good idea. Even educated speakers are apt to read with a different pronunciation from that in their normal speech. You can usually get a more natural pronunciation by giving a prompt in English, or an equivalent in the contact language being used, and then having the speakers respond by saying the required word in their own language. (You should use a technique like this even when working on English.) Other useful elicitation techniques include naming objects in pictures. One linguist I know always travels with books about the birds, mammals and insects in the region. Children's reading books often have useful illustrations. But you should note that elderly speakers in some countries may not be accustomed to looking at pictures. I remember one old man in Kenya who had no trouble naming the animals represented by crude carvings that are sold to tourists, but could not recognize those same animals in well-drawn pictures.

There are some excellent materials for speech pathologists that can be used equally well for eliciting words from speakers who are not in need of therapy. Most of the web sites I am familiar with were devised for speakers of English, but they can often be used with speakers of other languages. For example, Black Sheep Press, http://www.blacksheep-epress.com/pages/freebies, has freely download-able pictures that can be used for eliciting verbs, adjectives, preposi-tions, emotions, etc. Another site with many free pictures and stories designed for speech pathologists is: http://www.speechteach.co.uk/p_general/downloads.htm. You can also search for images at http://www.google.com/ (click on 'Images' at the top of the page, instead of accepting the default 'Web'), although you should remember when doing this that many of the images you find may be copyright. The web is full of sites that you can use to build up elicitation materials.

Illustrations can often be built into a story. Alternatively, if you want to make sure you get certain words pronounced, a map task is useful. Given a map such as that in figure 1.2, a request to explain how to get to the Holiday Inn on the route shown will produce

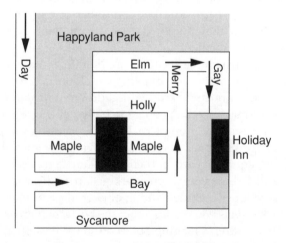

Figure 1.2   An example of a map task for eliciting specific words.

utterances like: 'Go down Day Street, turn left on Bay, left on Merry, right on Elm, and right on Gay.' This includes the words *bay*, *day*, *gay* in roughly comparable contexts (they would be more comparable if *gay* were not paragraph final).

Whatever the technique that is used for making a recording, each session should begin with an announcement of the date and time, the name of the person responsible for the recording, the place and topic of the recording session, an identification of the first speaker, and the speaker giving permission to be recorded (and permission to be identified, if that is the case). Whenever there is a new speaker this person should be identified, permissions recorded, and the time noted. All this information should also be written on the box for the tape, and, in an abbreviated form, on a label on the tape itself. Remember that labels come off, and that tapes get put in the wrong boxes, so make a point of recording all the information at the beginning of the tape. If anything changes during the course of the recording session, make a note of that as you go along, and sum up all the changes in a recorded comment at the end. Say what is happening clearly and distinctly into the microphone, so that the tape itself provides all the information you will need about the session. You can always edit out unwanted comments later.

When a recording session is over, or the tape is full, there are two things that should be done promptly, in addition to completing the documentation. First, secure your recordings, making it impossible to record anything else on top by accident. If you are using a cassette tape recorder, break the tabs on the back edge of the cassette. With a DAT recorder you have to move the slider to the locked position. In the case of a recording made directly onto a computer, make sure that the file is locked. Secondly, make a backup of the whole session, and store it in a safe place, preferably in a different location from the original recording. CDs on which you can write only once are invaluable for this purpose; but it really does not matter in what way you make a backup copy, as long as you do it some way.

1.5   Digital Recording

We should follow the previous section on making recordings by a short note on the choices that are available when using a DAT recorder or recording onto a computer. This is not the place for a full discussion on the nature of digital recording – you can find that in my book *Elements of Acoustic Phonetics*. All we need to note here is that computers, and to some extent DAT recorders, let you choose the range of frequencies you record. The highest frequency (pitch) that you can record depends on the sample rate – the number of points on the sound wave that are recorded as digital values every second. If you record a sound wave by writing its value onto the computer 22,000 times a second (that is, if the sample rate is 22,000 Hz), then you will (at least in theory) be recording frequencies up to 11,000 Hz. If your sample rate is 44,000 Hz (the same as a hi-fi CD), the theoretical limit is 22,000 Hz, which is above the limits of hearing for nearly everybody. As we saw earlier, speech recordings should include all frequencies up to 11,000 Hz (a sample rate of 22,000 Hz) but there is seldom any need to go higher.

My normal practice is to use a sample rate of 22,000 Hz when recording directly onto a computer for making a backup copy. When transferring data onto a computer for acoustic analysis a lower sample rate is often preferable, both because it saves space on the computer and because, curiously enough (see *Elements of Acoustic Phonetics*), it may enable you to make *more* accurate analyses of the most important phonetic aspects of sounds. All the information in vowels is below 5,000 Hz, which can be successfully recorded with a sample rate of 11,000 Hz; furthermore, the best analyses of the pitch of the voice can be made using this rate and eliminating the higher frequencies.

1.6   Listening to Recordings

I have already mentioned that it is best to make a rough transcription, perhaps in orthography, as soon as possible. Even if you don't have time to make a full transcription, at least listen to the whole recording, and make notes of what happened at particular times. Nowadays I do all my listening on a computer. There are many different programs that can be used to record and play speech on a computer. Some of them are available free or come with the operating system, but the better ones are fully supported commercial programs. In this book I will be referring to the one I use most often, PCquirer/Macquirer (the same program for different computers).

If the original recording was not made directly onto the computer, begin by copying sections of a minute or so onto your hard disk. You

When Daniel Jones, the greatest phonetician of the first part of the twentieth century, was setting out on a fieldwork trip, a reporter asked him, 'Professor Jones, what instruments are you taking with you?' He pointed to his ears and said, 'Only these.' There is no doubt that the ultimate authority in all phonetic questions is the human ear. But nowadays instrumental aids can often illuminate particular points, acting like a magnifying glass when we need to distinguish between two similar sounds.

can then listen to a word or a phrase at a time over headphones (computer loudspeakers are seldom very high quality), playing it over and over again with a single keystroke. If your computer system will allow you to listen to the recording at half speed without halving the pitch (as it should), then listen to vowels and diphthongs in this way. Consonants are best heard by playing the syllables containing them over and over again, but vowel quality can be fully appreciated when played at half speed without distortion. You should also try playing a selected portion of a sound in reverse. This allows you to focus more easily on offglides, which will have been made to sound like onsets.

When you think that you know how to represent a particular piece of a recording, transcribe it directly on the computer screen above the waveform, as well as adding it to the text, which you should be continually building up. I also try to get a group of consultants to listen to as much of the recording as possible. They can be a great help in checking the data. They are apt to say things like 'Listen to Charlie and how he says [the word for "grass"]. None of the rest of us say it like that.'

While you are checking your recordings, remember the object of the whole enterprise – to make a description of the sounds of a group of speakers. As a result of making a list of items to record you will know a great deal about the language. Now is the time to think about how you are going to write up your results. What are the most interesting points about this language? What are you going to discuss first?

It may seem odd to be thinking that far ahead, and no doubt your original outline will bear only a faint resemblance to what you finally write about the language. But all the time you are working you should remember the ultimate aim. You are not making recordings for your own collection, but planning how to describe the phonetic structures of a language. To do this effectively, write everything up as you go, getting as much down in well-ordered thoughts as you can, and certainly having a draft of the main points well before finishing the fieldwork.

1.7   Making Field Notes

Consideration of writing leads naturally to the final point to be discussed in this chapter. Coming back from the field with a set of well-labeled recordings is not enough. You must also have a written record of all that occurred. Before the days of computers it was easy to say how that should be accomplished. Buy the best notebook you can afford and write down everything that happened in pen. As soon as I was doing funded research, I bought leather-bound notebooks with numbered pages. Everything went in there: the date and time, the names of the speakers and other people present, their ages and relevant details of their linguistic background, and the word lists with glosses and transcriptions, always using the International Phonetic Alphabet, with varying degrees of detail being shown, and extra comments clarifying the precise use of the symbols. If some notes got made on scraps of paper, they were stuck in securely. Photographs of the speakers, photocopies of data from elsewhere, everything was dated and pasted in, so that there was a complete record of all that I was learning and observing. When I went back and made further notes on the data, I used a different color pen, leaving the original entries readable and adding a date for the notes in a different color.

To keep this book honest, I must admit that I tried to follow these procedures, but I was not always as thorough as I should have been.

Shortly after I went to UCLA I was hired as a consultant on the movie *My Fair Lady*. My job was to help Rex Harrison act like a Professor of Phonetics, pointing to the correct symbols and making transcriptions in appropriate notebooks. I explained that I was only a poor Assistant Professor of Phonetics, but if I were rich enough to have a butler and three singing maids, I would have handmade notebooks bound in green leather. Six such notebooks were made to my specification. Rex Harrison took one look at them and decided they were too big to go into his pocket. So I got a set of good notebooks for my own use.

I've just been looking back at my notebooks, which date from 1957 to the present. I see that there are errors – missing dates, full names of speakers not given, and some things not stuck in as well as they should have been. But my intentions were always to keep as full a record as possible.

Even with their failings, my notebooks have proved invaluable. When someone walks into my office and asks if I know anything about a particular language, say Shona, I can recall that I was in Zimbabwe in 1965 (it was called Southern Rhodesia then) and find what I had recorded – amongst other things, the word for a sugar ant, [sʷosʷe], with its unusual whistling fricatives that at the time I symbolized [sʷ] with some additional notes and pictures.

With the advent of computers it is not so clear how one should keep written records of a fieldwork investigation. I find it easiest to develop a word list on a computer, using a spreadsheet or a standard word-processing program. I like the ability to have transcriptions in an IPA font in one column, English glosses in a standard font in another, Swahili or whatever inter-language is being used in a third, and additional notes as needed elsewhere. That way I can alphabetize columns as needed, search for particular items, and add extra columns when working with a different speaker. But speakers sometimes find it distracting if you work on a computer while obtaining data. You need to make it clear to your speakers that you are fully focused on what they are saying. Making notes using pen and paper seems less intrusive. My compromise solution is to prepare word lists and notes on a computer, print them out, and then annotate them by hand while working with a speaker. At the end of the day I rename the data file (so that I always retain my older work), type in the new data that I have obtained, and print out the new files. Fortunately small printers are now cheap and can easily be used in the field.

The disadvantage of this method is that I end up with masses of printouts, and other loose pieces of paper, something that I previously tried to avoid. I put everything connected with a particular investigation into a single binder, instead of into one notebook. At the moment I find the data is as easily accessible as in my old notebooks, but I am not sure if this is really the best solution. However I am sure that permanent records should be in the form of printouts, not computer disks or CDs. I see no reason to believe that our current computer media will be readily accessible in 50, or even 20, years' time. But printed matter in English has been around for well over 500 years, and I expect it to be readable for many years in the future.

1.8   Instrumental Phonetic Techniques

For the first half of the last century phoneticians relied simply on their ears to make impressionistic descriptions of languages in the field. During the second half of the century their lives became easier because they could make tape recordings to support their auditory analyses. They could also take these recordings back into the lab for later acoustic analysis. But it was not until the latter part of the last century that it became possible to use a range of instrumental techniques in the field. Early phoneticians did wonderful work relying simply on their ears, but they could not find out what was going on inside a person's mouth, nor measure the amount of air flowing out of the nose in the ways we will discuss in the next two chapters. Nowadays you can take a basic phonetics lab – the kind of instrumentation that should be available to any student describing a language or dialect – anywhere you can carry a backpack. Instrumental phonetics has made it possible to document descriptions of languages more precisely. We can now

One of my tasks when working as an advisor on *My Fair Lady* was to help set up a 1910-style phonetics laboratory. We had an old-fashioned kymograph, a device with a revolving drum covered with white glossy paper that had been smoked so that there was a layer of soot on it. The subject of the experiment, Eliza Doolittle (Audrey Hepburn) spoke into a tube that led to a rubber drum that vibrated when a voiced sound was produced. A straw with a pointer on the end picked up these vibrations and made a trace on the soot-covered paper. It was quite an effective way of recording the duration of a voiced sound, but smoking the paper (and varnishing it afterwards so that it became fixed) was an elaborate procedure. I knew all about this technique as I am old enough to have used it as an undergraduate. I still have the records (one of which is reproduced below) of an undergraduate experiment in which I measured vowel length.

use scientific methodology to say how a previously undocumented contrast in a language is made. We can make hypotheses about the sounds of a language, and test them by making valid, reliable and significant measurements.

Let's consider what each of the terms, valid, reliable and significant, mean. Supposing, for example, that we had a hypothesis that there are two sets of vowels in English, one set exemplified by the vowels in *bait, beat, bite, boat, beaut(y)* and the other by the vowels in *bat, bet, bit, bob, bud.* (I've purposely used the way a schoolteacher might talk about the sounds of the letters 'A, E, I, O, U'.) We might make a hypothesis that the vowels in the first set are longer than those in the second. If we measured the vowel lengths in a recording of someone saying those words we would not have *valid* numbers for testing our hypothesis. These words differ in more than their vowels. They differ in their final consonants and number of syllables. We need an exact set of minimal pairs to make valid measurements that test the hypothesis, otherwise we can't be sure that the other differences between the words are not the reason for the differences in length.

Making *reliable* measurements means making them in accordance with a known procedure that others can follow. As we will see in chapter 4, measuring duration is not as simple a process as you might imagine. There are decisions to be made that have to be made explicit about where a sound begins and ends. Your measurements will not be considered reliable if others cannot follow your procedures and get the same answers.

Finally, for the hypothesis to be verified the measurements have to show that there is a *significant* difference. This requires showing that the differences are not due to chance. If you have measured a sufficient number of speakers to make sure that you are describing properties of the language, and not just the personal characteristics of one or two people, you will be able to report the statistical significance, the likelihood that the event is not due to chance. This book is not the appropriate place for a discussion of statistical techniques for measuring significance, but you should bear in mind that if you want to make claims about a language or a dialect, you should always subject them to statistical tests. Much of the rest of this book will be concerned with making measurements of speech by instrumental means. Try to make sure that these measurements are always valid, reliable, and statistically significant.

2

Finding the Places of Articulation

2.1 Still and Video Photography

When someone says *fie* and *vie*, you can see that the lower lip approaches the upper teeth for the **f** and **v**. The subtle differences between the labiodental fricatives **f** and **v** and their bilabial counterparts ɸ and β can be photographed. Figure 2.1 illustrates contrasts of this kind in Logba, a Niger-Congo language spoken in Ghana. These photographs of the consonants in the words ùβà 'measles' and ùvá 'side' were taken with a still camera, and hence had to be carefully timed. The camera took five frames in a second, so, in the course of a few trials, it was possible to catch appropriate moments in the articulation. A recording was made at the same time, making it possible to hear the clicks of the camera shutter, and find a photograph that was taken in the middle of the consonant. Pulling the tape slowly past the head by hand enabled one to hear a low-pitched, slowed-down version of the word on which the clicks of the shutter were clearly apparent. Thankfully we can now check whether the camera clicks were in the right place much more easily by displaying the waveform on a computer.

You can also avoid many timing problems altogether by using a video camera, which provides by far the easiest way of taking photographs of lip and jaw movements. (As I noted in chapter 1, video cameras are also useful in that they can be used as backup audio recording devices, helping you out when you've dropped your DAT recorder in a river.) Nowadays I nearly always use a video camera for photographs of lip positions. There is still the problem that a video is a succession of shots taken at a rate of 24 per second, so you have to be

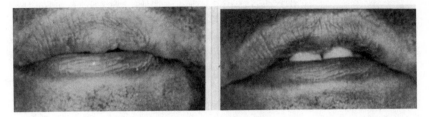

Figure 2.1   The lip positions in the consonants in two Logba words, **ùβà** 'measles' and **ùvá** 'side'.

Figure 2.2   Adjusting a mirror so that it is possible to see full and side face views of a speaker from Niue (South Pacific).

sure that the lip position you are photographing does not change appreciably in a 40 ms interval.

You can get another view of the lips by taking simultaneous front and side views, holding a mirror against the side of the face (or, preferably, getting someone else to do it, so that you can operate the camera). Adjust the mirror so that it is possible to see full-face and side views at the same time. If you are using a video camera, you can take a wide shot first as in figure 2.2, and then zoom in so that you have the best possible picture of the lips.

If you use a digital video camera you will be able to transfer the images directly into a computer, and then move through them one at a time. Video cameras provide images at a rate of 24 frames per second, which is fast enough for most speech movements. The fastest the lips can be moved together and apart (other than in a labial trill) is about six times a second. Tongue tip movements can be slightly faster. You cannot guarantee that you have a single image recording the maximum extent of a rapid movement, but it won't be far off. Video is not fast enough to record the small rapid movements in a labial trill, which are caused by aerodynamic forces rather than by muscular movements. In a trill the lips vibrate at around 20 to 30 movements per second, which is much the same speed as the frame rate. The same applies to a tongue tip trill. You can record the raising of the tip of the tongue to make a contact, and you can even see when the tongue is vibrating. But you cannot record the individual vibrations. We will return to the question of studying trills when we consider acoustic techniques.

Figure 2.3 shows pictures of a speaker of Isoko, a Niger-Congo language spoken in Nigeria, photographed with a camera taking 5 frames per second. Taking good photographs of people with dark skin tones requires expert lighting, something one often can't provide, as the choice may be between bright sunlight, which produces high contrasts, or a dark hut, in which not much is visible. If you have not been able to take well-lit photographs, you can make the boundaries of the lips stand out by trimming the photographs as shown in figure 2.3.

The photographs in this figure provide good documentation of some interesting contrasts. Isoko has three labial consonants that contrast in the words ɛʋɛ́ 'breath', ɛ́vɛ́ 'how' and ɛɣʷɛ́ 'hoe'. The photograph at the top shows the vowel, which is the same in each of these words. In the second photograph, taken during the consonant in the middle of the word ɛʋɛ́, it is apparent that the consonant ʋ involves only a very small gesture of the lips, which are only slightly more approximated than in the vowel in the first photograph. The third photograph shows the more commonly found consonant v, in the word 'ɛ́vɛ́', in which the lower lip is close to the upper teeth. The last photograph shows a rounded velar fricative ɣʷ. This sound has a different tongue position, which, of course, cannot be seen in these photographs; however, the very close approximation of the lips is clear.

In addition to a video camera, I now travel with a digital camera and a small computer printer that will print color photographs. This is very helpful in many ways. It replaces the Polaroid camera I used in

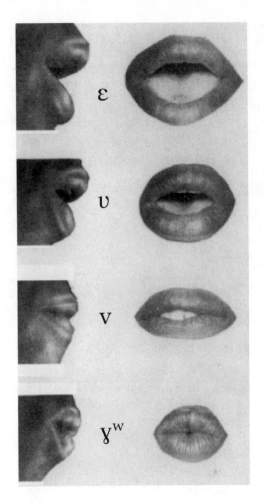

Figure 2.3   Photographs of a speaker of Isoko. The top photograph shows the position of the lips during the vowel ɛ́. The other three photographs show the position during the consonants in ɛ́υɛ́ 'breath', ɛ́vɛ́ 'how' and ɛ́ɣʷɛ́ 'hoe'.

earlier fieldwork. One of the gifts that people appreciate most is a photograph of themselves. After being given a photo, speakers may be willing to go on working for another couple of hours. I also keep photographs of speakers for my own records. When listening to a recording of Banawa, a language spoken in the Amazonian rain forest,

Figure 2.4 A Banawa speaker with his son.

it is useful to have a reminder that speaker 3 was the one shown in figure 2.4, who was carrying his small son.

2.2 Basic Palatography

Video cameras are helpful for recording movements of the lips and changes in jaw position, but they are of little help in telling us what part of the tongue is involved in an articulation and where the articulation is made on the roof of the mouth. The best way of recording this kind of data in the field (or in a simple laboratory set-up) is by means of palatography, a nineteenth-century technique that has now been developed so that it is capable of providing a great deal of information on tongue gestures.

Fieldwork palatography involves painting the tongue with a black substance, asking the speaker to say a word containing the articulation to be studied, and then observing where the black substance has been transferred onto the roof of the mouth. By putting a mirror into the

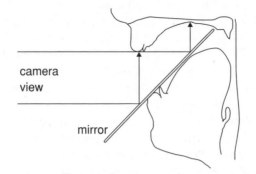

Figure 2.5   A system for photographing the roof of the mouth. The arrows show how (ideally) the view from the camera is directly up into the roof of the mouth.

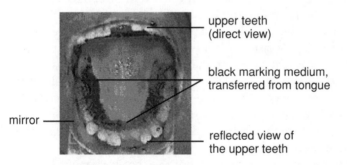

Figure 2.6   Palatogram of an Arrernte **t**. (Photograph by Victoria Anderson.)

mouth you can see (and photograph) the whole of the upper surface as illustrated in figure 2.5.

Figure 2.6 shows a photograph using this system, taken by Victoria Anderson as part of her fieldwork on Arrernte, an aboriginal language of Australia. The speaker's upper teeth are at the top of the picture. Below them, reflected in the mirror, is a view of the roof of the mouth, with the inside of the upper teeth being at the bottom of the picture. The speaker had had his tongue painted before saying a word containing an alveolar stop. The marking medium has been transferred to an area all the way around the molar teeth and across the alveolar ridge behind the upper front teeth (one of which is missing). This palatogram does not provide any information on the movements of the tongue, but we can see where in the mouth the stop was made.

The best marking medium is a mixture of equal parts olive oil and powdered charcoal. Powdered charcoal is completely tasteless and available from a pharmacist (it is used in medicines for flatulence). Any edible cooking oil will do. Paint the mixture on the part of the tongue that is likely to be used in the articulation, using a thick paint-brush. Remember that you don't know exactly what part of the tongue will be used in a particular articulation, and it is better to cover more than less. Be sure to go far enough back. You may have to paint not only the tip of the tongue but also the underside of the tip if there is any chance of a retroflex articulation being used.

Tell the speaker to relax and not swallow after the tongue has been painted. You want a natural pronunciation of the word, which most speakers can achieve once they have found that the mixture in their mouth is not unpleasant. Turn on the video camera so that you are recording everything, ask for the word to be spoken, put a mirror in the mouth and photograph the contact areas. You will need to shine a light into the mouth so that it can be photographed without any shadows. It is best to have a proper light attached to the camera, but even a flashlight is better than nothing. After each word has been photographed and the camera switched off, the mouth should be rinsed with water mixed with a little lemon juice so as to clean the upper surface. Then you can repeat the sequence with the next word: paint, relax, start video recording, speaker says the word, head back, mirror in the mouth, photograph.

Practice putting the mirror into the speaker's mouth before you do any painting of the tongue. Get the speaker to open the mouth as wide as possible. Then slip the mirror in so that its edge is behind the upper back teeth. Most speakers tilt their heads forwards at this moment and

---

Part of the joy of palatography is that it is possible to improvise and get some data without being too elaborate. At a party I once met a speaker of Basque who said that he distinguished a dental s̪ from an alveolar s, a distinction I wanted to observe. I borrowed a small hand mirror, and made some charcoal by burning a piece of toast and scraping the black parts onto a flat surface. I ground them into a fine powder using a beer bottle as a rolling-pin. There was some olive oil in the kitchen to mix with the powder, and a cotton swab served as a paintbrush. Lacking a camera, I looked into his mouth and sketched what I could see. An interesting evening's work. The beer was good, too.

do not open their mouths wide enough. You want the head tilted back, the mouth wide open and the jaw pulled back. Then you can place the mirror at an angle of 45° to the plane of the upper teeth, so that the camera sees a view equivalent to looking straight up at the roof of the mouth, as shown in figure 2.5. The mirror should be about 5 cm wide and 15 cm long. A local glassworks can cut and bevel the edges of a mirror of this sort.

Making palatographic investigations requires a great deal of sensitivity to local customs. In many parts of Asia it is not appropriate for a man to place his hand on the top of a young woman's head. When putting a mirror into someone's mouth, make sure that you ask permission to steady the head with your other hand before beginning. It is always helpful to keep a polite distance away from the speaker. With a video camera and a zoom lens it is possible to take a picture of just the mirror in the mouth from a meter or so away, which speakers may find easier than having the photographer too close.

As with any instrumental procedure, you should demonstrate the whole procedure on yourself first. You can paint your own tongue quite easily, using a mirror. You can then relax, say a word, put the mirror into your mouth and let the speaker see the roof of your mouth. Make it clear that you have your own paintbrush, and that you have a separate paintbrush and a cleaned mirror for each speaker. I use a number of different color paintbrushes, cheap ones made for children rather than artists. I also pour a little of the oil and charcoal mixture into a saucer for each speaker so that they see that each paintbrush is dipped into a separate container. You must be careful with the black oil and charcoal mixture. It stains clothes easily, so it is best to put a towel or old shirt around the speaker. You should also make sure that the speaker sees that the mirrors have been thoroughly cleaned and stored in a sterilizing solution.

The words used in a palatographic investigation have to be carefully chosen. Palatography records the contacts that have been made in the whole word. When investigating the difference between English s and ʃ, it is no good looking at words like *sin* and *shin*. The contact for the n at the end of the word will obscure the contacts in the s and ʃ. A more suitable pair would be *sip* and *ship*. You need to search for words that have only the consonants you are interested in, or in which the only other consonants are bilabials or glottal stops. Sometimes this is not possible and you have to use a word containing a velar consonant. This may not be too bad if you are investigating dental consonants,

> Indians are very quick to notice if something that has been in one per-
> son's mouth is then dipped into a common pot. An Indian friend once
> told me how horrified he was the first time he went to dinner in an
> American household. His host was making soup. Every now and then she
> would taste it to see if it needed more seasoning – and then put the
> spoon, which had been in her mouth, back into the pot. Despite his
> admiration for her, my Indian friend found it difficult to eat dinner.

but it probably will affect the tongue position. Also remember that
vowel and consonant articulations interact. Don't compare words like
she and *saw*, as the high front vowel of *she* will cause noticeable raising
of the sides of the tongue in comparison with *saw*. As we noted in the
first chapter, always try to investigate minimal pairs, like *she* and *sea*,
or *Shaw* and *saw*.

We usually want to know not only what part of the roof of the
mouth is involved in the investigation, but also what part of the tongue
has been used. We can get this information by reversing the process.
Paint the roof of the mouth. Get the speaker to relax with the mouth
slightly open (so that you can see that the tongue is not touching the
roof of the mouth), start the video camera, and ask the speaker to
say the word and then open the mouth and let the tongue lie in a
neutral position on the lower lip (this requires a little practice). After
the photograph has been taken, the speaker should thoroughly cleanse
the tongue, perhaps using water with a little lemon juice in it, and
wipe it with a paper towel or a cloth. It is much more difficult to clean
the tongue than the roof of the mouth.

Photographs of the tongue made in this way are called linguograms. They are never likely to be as comparable as photographs
of the roof of the mouth. It is difficult to place the tongue in exactly
the same position after every utterance. But you can usually see whether
it is the blade of the tongue that has been used for a laminal articulation or the tip (or even the underside of the tip) for an apical (or
a retroflex) articulation. If you are investigating a potential retroflex
articulation, the tip of the tongue will have to be raised before being
photographed.

Figure 2.7 shows the palatogram of Arrernte **t** in figure 2.6, this time
with its associated linguogram. Below it there is another palatogram
and linguogram, in this case of Arrernte **tʃ** spoken by the same speaker,
and also photographed by Victoria Anderson. On both palatograms

an arbitrary grid has been drawn, based on the teeth and other anatomical landmarks, so that it is possible to compare one palatogram
with another. In the palatogram of **t** in the upper part of the figure the
tongue contact is on the forward part of the alveolar ridge, about 8
mm in front of the arbitrary reference line. The affricate **t͡ʃ** in the lower
palatogram involved an articulatory contact that was further back,
only about 4 mm from the reference line. The sides of the tongue
made contact higher in the palate in the lower palatogram, as is shown
by the fact that the untouched part of the horizontal reference line
is shorter. Both these points can be measured with reference to the
imposed grid.

It is difficult to make reliable measurements of the contacts on
the tongue, shown in the linguograms on the right, as the shape of the
tongue is not constant. The upper linguogram shows that the tip of
the tongue is used to make the alveolar stop. In the lower picture, it is

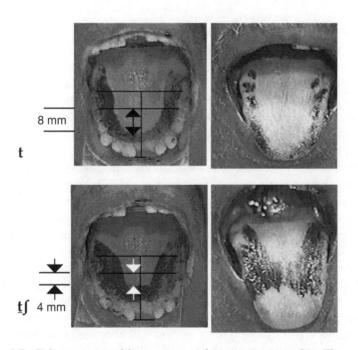

Figure 2.7   Palatograms and linguograms of an Arrernte speaker. The
arrows indicate the distance between the back of the tongue contact near
the center of the mouth and an arbitrary reference line. (Photographs by
Victoria Anderson.)

apparent that the blade of the tongue is used for the palatoalveolar affricate, as the tip of the tongue is completely free of any of the black marking medium. But, because the shapes of the tongue in the two photographs are not the same, no measurements can be made. Pictures of the tongue can be compared only qualitatively, noting, for example, that one articulation involves the tip of the tongue and the other the posterior part of the blade.

Palatography is a fairly slow process. It can take an hour or more to photograph half a dozen words – two pictures for each word, one of the tongue and another of the roof of the mouth. Many speakers feel that that is enough for one session. Palatographic investigations should be planned carefully, allowing enough time to get sufficient words from as many speakers as possible. As with all phonetic studies, there will be more variation between speakers than within repetitions by the same speaker, so it is important to photograph a number of different people.

2.3   More Elaborate Palatography

Much more information can be gained from palatograms and linguograms if you know the shape of the roof of the mouth. Many sounds are distinguished, for example, by whether the tongue contacts the anterior or posterior part of the alveolar ridge, making the difference between an alveolar or retroflex sound. Photographs of the roof of the mouth, such as those on the left-hand side of figure 2.7, do not show exactly where the alveolar ridge is. For that you need an outline of the sagittal section, similar to that used in many diagrams of articulations. You can make this quite easily in the field using dental impression material. Figure 2.8 shows a speaker of !Xóõ having an impression of his mouth made in the Kalahari Desert.

Dental impression material is available from any dental supply house. I like the kind that changes color. It is purple when you mix it with water, pink when it is ready to be put into the mouth, and green when it is set, so that it can be taken out. You will also need a rubber mixing bowl and a spatula to mix the material thoroughly.

You do not need to make as full an impression as a dentist usually makes, using a tray that fits around both sides of the teeth. All we are interested in are the inner surfaces of the teeth. When you have mixed

Figure 2.8   Making an impression of the shape of the roof of the mouth in the Kalahari Desert.

the material according to the directions on the packet, take a large mound of it (about the amount recommended for making a full upper jaw impression) and place it on the mirror that you use when photographing the upper surface of the mouth. Ask the speaker to open the mouth and lean forward while you put the mirror in and press it against the lower surface of the upper teeth. You can get the speaker to bite down (gently) on the mirror, so that it is held firmly in place. Use sufficient material so that you get the shape of the whole of the oral cavity, including the soft palate. As the speaker has to breathe while the material is setting, the soft palate will be lowered 1–2 mm, but this will affect only the very back part of the roof of the mouth. Some of the material will be pushed out of the mouth. This excess material should be allowed to set around the upper lip, so that you can get this shape too. Speakers often drool a lot, which is why they should lean forward, but this does not affect the setting process. When the change of color indicates that the material is ready to be removed, rock the mirror slightly to loosen the material and then take it out.

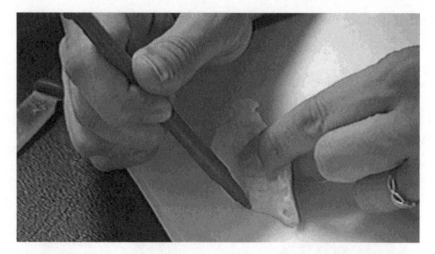

Figure 2.9 Victoria Anderson tracing an impression of the palate that has been cut in half so as to obtain part of a sagittal view of the speaker's vocal organs.

Making dental impressions is not difficult, but it does require practice. You have to be sure that the material goes right up to the roof of the mouth, that it goes far enough back, and that it covers all the inside surfaces of the teeth. Practice making impressions of your own mouth until you have made one that looks perfect.

If you simply want to know the shape of the mid-sagittal section of the palate, you can get this by cutting the impression material in half, and tracing the edges as shown in figure 2.9. However, you may want to make a more elaborate map of the palate, and for this purpose you should make a plaster cast of the impression material, so that you have a more permanent record of the speaker's mouth shape. Unless you keep it under water, the alginate impression material will soon shrink and lose its shape.

You can buy plaster for making a model of the speaker's palate from any hardware store. Get the hard, stone-like, type, which takes longer to set but is much more durable. Put water in your rubber mixing bowl and then add a little plaster (do it in this order) using a spatula to mix it thoroughly. Go on adding powder to the water until, after spatulating thoroughly, you have a thick, creamy mixture. Put the alginate impression into a small plastic bowl such as a margarine

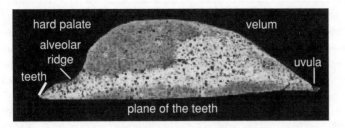

Figure 2.10   Part of a copy produced by placing half of an impression of the palate on the glass of a copy machine. Labels added later.

container, with the roof of the mouth uppermost, then pour the plaster onto it. Tap the bowl against the table continuously, so as to remove air bubbles (dental labs use a special vibrating table for this purpose). When the plaster is hard, take it out of the bowl, and remove the impression material. You will have a good permanent record of the speaker's palate. You can always trace the midline of this palate by putting additional impression material into it, letting it set, and then cutting it in half and tracing it as shown in figure 2.9. Alternatively, you can take the cut half of the impression and place it on the glass of a copying machine. This will produce an image such as that in figure 2.10 (without, of course, the labels, which I added later). This impression of my mouth was produced while the soft palate was lowered (so that I could breathe through my nose). It shows the shape of the roof of my mouth during a nasal rather than a stop.

Figure 2.11 shows three palatograms produced by a speaker of Scottish Gaelic. These palatograms differ from those we have been discussing in two ways. Firstly, instead of being painted with an oily black mixture that gets transferred onto the roof of the mouth, the tongue was kept clean. A black powder, a mixture of powdered charcoal and a little drinking chocolate (for flavor, and to keep the speaker salivating slightly) was sprayed onto the roof of the mouth. When a word was spoken, part of the powder was wiped away by the tongue contacting the roof of the mouth. So in this kind of palatogram, the black area is where the tongue has *not* touched. The principle is the same, but the black/non-black areas are reversed. The second point to note about these palatograms is that the mirror was not at an angle of 45° to the camera and the line of the upper teeth. As a result, the front-to-back dimension is lengthened in relation to the side-to-side

The photographs in figure 2.11 are part of a study by Fred Macaulay, a classmate of mine at Edinburgh University. Almost 45 years after taking this set of photographs of his own pronunciation of Gaelic he was kind enough to go to his local dentist and get a cast made, which he sent to me. He has lost a few teeth since making the palatograms, but the shape of his palate has not altered. Fred is a Gaelic speaker from South Uist in the Hebrides. He did not speak English at all until he went to school.

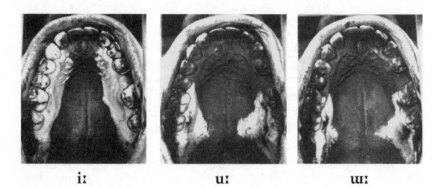

iː   uː   ɯː

Figure 2.11   Palatograms of the Scottish Gaelic vowels as in the words iː, i, 'she, her', uː, *thu*, 'you' (sing.) and ɯː, *aodh*, 'liver'.

dimension. This was done deliberately so as to be able to record contact areas in the back of the mouth.

You can get even more information from these and other palatograms if you make the photographs life-size, so that they can be compared directly with a cast of the palate. A standard computer drawing program was used to transform the dimensions of the photographs in figure 2.11 independently. The side-to-side distance between the molar teeth on the two sides of the mouth was made the same as this distance on the cast of the speaker's mouth. Similarly, the front-to-back distance between the front teeth and a line between the posterior molars was made to be the same as on the cast. The resulting photographs are shown in figure 2.12.

The palatograms in figure 2.12 have white lines added, showing points that are 5, 10 and 12.5 mm down from the highest point of the palate. There are several techniques that can be used to find these

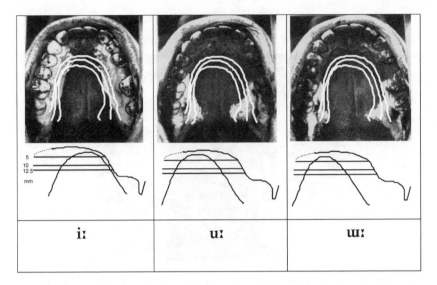

Figure 2.12   Re-scaled palatograms with contour lines superimposed and sagittal sections showing estimates of the tongue positions in the Gaelic vowels in figure 2.11.

contour lines representing the height of different parts of the roof of the mouth. One is to make an impression as discussed above, and then, instead of cutting it vertically as demonstrated in figure 2.9, make horizontal slices, each a few millimeters apart. Tracing around the slices provides the appropriate contours. A more accurate way is to fill a cast with a black liquid, first to a depth of 2.5 mm, then to 5 mm, 7.5 mm and so on, each time taking a photograph of the filled cast. Figure 2.13 shows a cast filled to a depth of 7.5 mm. When the series of photographs has been put on a computer, the images can be enlarged and the edges of the fluid traced precisely. The traced contours can then be superimposed on the palatograms.

The same lines, 5, 10 and 12.5 mm down from the highest point of the palate, can be easily drawn on the sagittal sections, as shown in figure 2.12. Using these lines and the contours it is possible to estimate the shapes of the tongue that occurred in each vowel. In the first palatogram, the marking medium has been wiped away above all three lines in the center of the mouth, indicating that the sides of the tongue must have gone within 5 mm of the roof of the mouth in this region. In the other two palatograms the contact area is further back. If

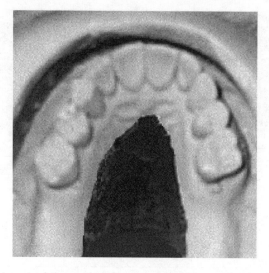

Figure 2.13   A cast of the roof of the mouth (filled to a depth of 7.5 mm).

we assume that the center of the tongue was slightly domed, making it a little higher than the sides, we can infer that the tongue shapes in these three vowels were approximately as shown in the sagittal sections in figure 2.12. The cast of the roof of the mouth did not extend as far back as the soft palate, so a dashed line has been drawn to indicate the sagittal section in that area.

Palatography is most helpful in studying consonants rather than vowels. A good example is provided by a set of data on Toda, a Dravidian language spoken in the Nilgiri Hills in India. Toda has four different sibilants exemplified by the words **koːṣ** 'money', **poːṣ** 'milk', **poːʃ** 'language', **poːṣ** (place name). (Toda is one of the comparatively few languages that has a larger number of contrasts at the ends of the syllables than at the beginning.) The palatograms of the words in figure 2.14 were made in the way described earlier in this chapter, first painting an oily black mixture on the tongue and photographing the black contact areas on the roof of the mouth, and then making another set of photographs, the linguograms, which were the result of painting the roof of the mouth and then photographing the black medium that had been transferred onto the tongue.

Two general points should be noted. Firstly, as we were interested only in articulations made in the front part of the mouth, we did not

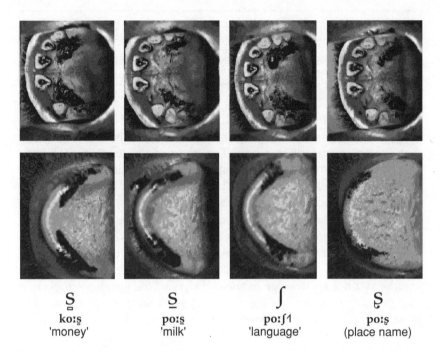

S̬̊
ko:s̬̊
'money'

S̱
po:s̱
'milk'

ʃ
po:ʃ1
'language'

ʂ
po:ʂ
(place name)

Figure 2.14 Palatograms and linguograms of four Toda words exemplifying the four voiceless fricatives in the language.

paint areas further back, nor did we try to photograph areas deep in the mouth. Speakers are always happier if they do not have to have their mouths wide open and a mirror placed deep inside. Secondly, all six of the Toda speakers we photographed had poor dentition, often missing several teeth. In addition, as they constantly chewed betel nuts, their teeth were very stained. The dark marks on the front teeth in all the photographs in figure 2.14 are stains, and not evidence of contact with the tongue. Photographs taken before making any palatograms can be useful in identifying permanent features such as these.

In the first word the tongue made contact with the roof of the mouth on the alveolar ridge, just behind the upper front teeth. There is no black on the tip of the tongue. When making these photographs we could see that the tip was down behind the lower front teeth in this word. We could also see that in the second word the tip was raised with, as the palatogram shows, the sides of the tongue making contact as far forward as the alveolar ridge. In the third word the contact was

> The Toda are a small minority group, living in reserved areas in the Nilgiri Hills in India. They have some famous temples, but we were too busy to visit them. I'm not much of a tourist, and found it more fun to talk to our friendly Toda speakers, who entertained us well.

not quite so far forward. In addition, the distance between the black areas at the right of the photograph (between the molars) is smaller than in the second photograph. The body of the tongue must have been raised up towards the roof of the mouth in this word. The final word has a retroflex consonant. The contact on the roof of the mouth was very far back, and there is hardly any black to be seen in the photograph of the tongue. Most of the tongue contact involved the underside of the tongue, which is not visible in this photograph.

We made casts of all our speakers' mouths. From a study of the palatograms and linguograms and direct observations of the speaker, together with a knowledge of the contours of the speaker's mouth, it was possible to infer that the four shapes of the tongue involved in these four fricatives were as shown in figure 2.15. The results were

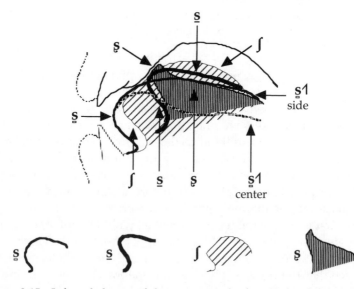

Figure 2.15   Inferred shapes of the tongue in the four Toda sibilants. For ṣ the solid line shows the sides of the tongue and the dashed line shows the center.

essentially the same for all six speakers. As I emphasized in the first chapter, it is always better to get data on a smaller set of words from many speakers than to conduct a massive study of a single speaker, who may or may not use articulations that are typical of the language.

2.4 Electropalatography

There are other systems of palatography. Dynamic electropalatography (EPG) is a valuable tool for showing changes in the contact areas on the roof of the mouth. This technique cannot be used in most field circumstances or for a one-time speaker in a lab, as it requires a special false palate to be made for each speaker. (Flexible palates that can be used by different speakers have been made, but are generally not very useful.) This palate has a number of contact points (96 in one system) that will record whenever they are touched by the tongue. It has to fit exactly into the speaker's palate and is fairly costly to make. Figure 2.16 shows the arrangement of the contact points and the wires connected to each of them, which eventually join together into two thicker wires that can come out at the sides of the mouth.

Dynamic EPG allows one to study movements and, given some additional programming, look at the palate from different angles. Pat

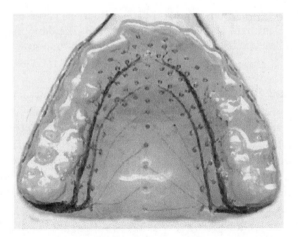

Figure 2.16 A false palate that fits inside a particular speaker's mouth. There are 96 electrodes connected by wires that join together into two thicker wires.

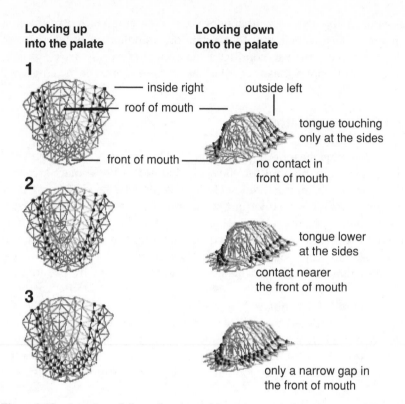

Figure 2.17   A series of three frames at 10 ms intervals based on work by Pat Keating, Dani Byrd and Cheng Cheng SawTan. The dark points are those that the tongue has contacted when moving up to form English **s**.

Keating, Dani Byrd and Cheng Cheng Saw Tan have produced a three-dimensional view of the palate illustrating various articulations. Figure 2.17 shows three frames from a video in which the tongue is moving up to form **s** at the beginning of the word *say*. You can see how, in articulating this sound, the sides of the tongue lower and the tip comes up to form a narrow channel on the alveolar ridge.

Once a custom-made palate is available, dynamic electropalatography can record several utterances in a short time. There is no need to clean the tongue and palate after every photograph, or to worry about overlapping contacts. This makes it possible to record sentences in which the same sound occurs in different contexts and to compare, for example, the articulation of **s** in *stop, sop, spot, toss, tops*, etc., a task that is impossible with direct palatography. But dynamic electropalatography also has its limitations. The expense and time required to make individual palates make it virtually impossible to use it for recording 10–12 speakers in the field, an easy task for direct palatography. In the future, better flexible palates that can be used by different speakers may be available, but they have not yet been adequately developed. In addition, electropalatography provides no information on the part of the tongue that is being used. You can't tell, for example, the difference between an apical (tongue tip) and a laminal (tongue blade) articulation. Nor can you record contacts on the soft palate, and, with many systems, contacts on the teeth are not recorded. Nevertheless, we must always remember that speech consists of movements of the vocal organs, and dynamic electropalatography records them in a way that reveals much about how people talk.

2.5   Further reading

Palatography

A general account of palatography:
Marchal, A. (1988) *La Palatographie*. Paris: CNRS.

Three studies, providing materal for this chapter, demonstrating the use of palatography:
Anderson, V. (2000). Connecting Phonetics and Phonology: Evidence from Western Arrernte. UCLA Ph.D. dissertation.
Dart, S. (1998). Comparing French and English coronal consonant articulation. *Journal of Phonetics*, 26(1), 71–94.
Spajic, S., Ladefoged, P., and Bhaskararao, P. (1996). The trills of Toda. *Journal of the International Phonetic Association*, 26(1), 1–21.

Electropalatography

Hardcastle, W. J., and Gibbon, F. E. (1997). Electropalatogaphy and its clinical applications. In M. J. Ball and C. Code (eds.), *Instrumental clinical phonetics*, pp. 149–93. London: Whurr Publishers.

A paper illustrating electropalatography:
Byrd, D. (1996). Influences on articulatory timing in consonant sequences. *Journal of Phonetics*, 24(2), 209–44.

3
Aerodynamic Investigations

3.1 Recording Air Pressure and Airflow

Palatography is a good way of defining the precise place of articulation of a sound, but it provides less information about how the sound was made. It will tell you, for example, that a given sound had an alveolar closure, but you cannot tell from a palatogram whether it was a stop or a nasal. To distinguish between these possibilities you need to know whether the air was coming out of the nose or not. You can usually tell this just by listening, without an instrumental investigation. But, as we will see, there are some more complicated cases in which it is useful to be able to record exactly when and how the air flows out of the mouth and the nose in making a particular sound.

We can also learn a lot from records of the pressure of the air. All speech involves pushing air out of the lungs with a certain degree of respiratory effort, with more effort being required for a stressed syllable than for an unstressed one. The extra effort increases the pressure of the air below the vocal folds (the subglottal pressure). If we find that this pressure is higher in one syllable rather than another, then it is likely that this syllable uses more respiratory effort and is a stressed syllable.

People sometimes confuse the notions of air pressure and airflow. One way of thinking about them is to consider what happens when you blow through a tube. If the tube has a closed tap at the other end you can blow as hard as you can (produce a great deal of pressure), but there will be no flow. Open the tap a little and, still blowing as hard as you can, there will be a small flow. When the tap is fully open

A few years ago, before we had laptop computers and pocket-sized tape recorders, a traveling phonetics lab was heavy and bulky. One needed a 30-pound ink-writing oscillograph to record air pressure and flow, and a Nagra tape recorder and accessories weighing more than 20 pounds, plus a palatography camera, impression material and film. All told, my equipment topped 80 pounds, without considering notebooks and clothes. When my wife came along with me she said she felt like a packhorse.

there will be a great deal of flow. The same pressure can result in very different flows, depending on the resistance to the flow.

Now consider what happens when you blow bubbles out of a tube immersed in water. If the end of the tube were deep under the surface, you would have to blow hard (use a high pressure) to get any bubbles, whereas if the tube (or straw in a soft-drink bottle) were only a centimeter or so down, you would need very little effort – only a low pressure – to produce bubbles. The pressure of the air is quite distinct from the rate of flow of the air. The tube may be just under the surface, so that very little pressure is required, but you can still blow bubbles at a slow or rapid rate. When the tube is deep below the surface you have to blow hard to produce any bubbles. If you want to produce a rapid stream of bubbles, you don't have to use any more pressure, you just have to push a greater volume of air out. The pressure is the push required to produce any bubbles at a particular depth of the tube. The rate of flow is akin to the number of bubbles per second.

Usually, when you increase the pressure the flow also increases, but this is not necessarily so. Later in this chapter we will consider records of breathy voice in which there is a greater flow but a lesser subglottal pressure. The relation between the air pressure and the airflow depends on the resistance to the flow, the magnitude of the obstruction to the outgoing air. When the resistance remains the same, an increase in pressure will cause an increase in flow. But when the resistance drops (as in, for example, breathy voice, when the vocal folds are further apart) the flow will increase without any increase in pressure. The lungs do not have to be pushed any harder to produce breathy voice. All that is required is for the vocal folds to come apart so that there is a greater flow of outgoing air.

Aerodynamic investigations of the airflow and air pressure require specialized equipment, but it is often available in even a small phonetics

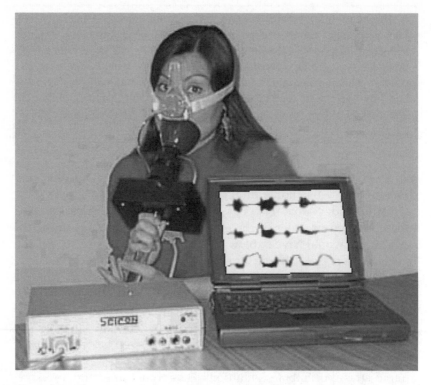

Figure 3.1   The system for recording air pressure and air flow described in the text.

laboratory. This equipment enables one to record the airflow from the mouth and nose. In addition it can record the pressure of the air in the front of the mouth and in the pharynx. The system I have been using is illustrated in figure 3.1. It consists of a small box (bottom left of the picture) connected to a laptop computer (bottom right), and an assembly with oral and nasal masks and pressure tubes held by the speaker, together with a microphone that records the sound.

The mask for capturing the oral airflow fits around the mouth and below the jaw. Above it the nasal airflow mask is fastened over the nose by a velcro band that goes around the head. Both masks are joined by small tubes to inputs on the assembly. Two other inputs are used for tubes, not visible in the photograph, for sensing the air pressure in the mouth and in the pharynx. This system, with two

Figure 3.2   A Bushman in the Kalahari Desert, inserting a tube through the nose into the pharynx.

pressures and two flows, is available from SciconRD.com. The current price (April 2003) is about $3,250; a system recording only one pressure and one flow channel would be about $2,500.

Recording the airflow requires talking while pressing the masks firmly against the face, making sure that there are no leaks. The easiest way to record the pressure of the air in the mouth is by speaking while using a small tube between the lips. You can sometimes get speakers to hold a thin tube between the lips, with its open end up near the hard palate. If the tube is small enough it will not interfere too much, even with alveolar stops such as **t**, **d**. Speakers will, however, find it hard to produce good fricatives, such as **s**, **ʃ**.

To make a recording of the pressure of the air behind a velar closure one needs a tube with its open end in the pharynx. The easiest way to do this (and it is not as difficult as you might imagine) is to pass a small tube through the nose as shown in figure 3.2. A suitable tube is an infant feeding tube, available from hospital supply centers in a sterile package. Push the tube gently but firmly into the nostril for about 8 cm, pointing it towards the back of the neck, and not upwards. The two principal mistakes that people make are to push the tube up

> One of my most embarrassing moments as a young post-doc was when I was showing the eminent Swedish phonetician, Gunnar Fant, how to pass a tube through the nose into the pharynx. I demonstrated on myself as usual, and then got him to try. He inserted the tube into his nostril and pushed hard for a long time, gamely struggling on, his eyes watering and his face red, all with no results. I peered into his pharynx, but nothing was visible. After he had pushed over 20 cm of the tube into his nose it finally appeared – out of the other nostril. I have made many recordings with tubes passed through the nose, and this is the only time that this has ever happened. Gunnar Fant tried again and made successful pressure recordings.

the nose instead of backward, and to be too tentative about the initial insertion. The entrance to the nasal passages is much more easily irritated than the part further back. Hold the tube between the thumb and forefinger about 8 cm from the tip, and simply push it straight back. If the tube has a natural curve, as it often does having been coiled up in a package, make sure the curve is pointing down. Once the tube is about 8 cm inside the nostril, you can go more slowly, pushing it in a centimeter at a time, and swallowing as you do so. If it appears to meet an obstruction, pull it back, twist it a little, and try pushing it in again, swallowing as you do so. People often gag slightly when the end of the tube comes round into the pharynx. This may be because it has been pushed too far down. If you look into the mouth, using a flashlight, you should be able to see the end of the tube just below the level of the uvula.

When recording air pressure in the mouth or in the pharynx, it is important to keep the tubes free of mucus. You can clear a tube that has been passed through the nose by connecting it to a syringe that will blow air through it. Even tubes that are between the lips need to be watched, as speakers often suck on them so that they tend to get filled with saliva. They should be blown clear at frequent intervals. The size of the tubes for recording pressure is another point that must be considered. If you want to record the changes in pressure and flow that occur as a result of the vibrations of the vocal folds, you will need to use tubes like an infant feeding tube with an internal diameter of at least 2 mm.

To record the pressure of the air associated with stressed as opposed to unstressed syllables we need to record the pressure below the vocal

Figure 3.3   A tracheal puncture for recording subglottal pressure.

folds. A true recording of the subglottal pressure can be made only by making a tracheal puncture. This is a procedure that must be performed by a physician. A local anesthetic is applied both externally and inside the trachea by means of a fine needle. A larger needle with an internal diameter of 2 mm can then be inserted between the rings of the trachea as shown in figure 3.3. As you can see from my face it is not at all painful. But it is not a procedure that can be carried out in fieldwork situations.

We can get some information on the subglottal pressure without a tracheal puncture. As a result of having recorded the pressure below the vocal folds by means of a tracheal puncture and that above them by using a small tube between the lips, we know that during voiceless stops such as **p** there is very little difference between the oral pressure and the subglottal pressure. When the vocal folds are apart, there is very little resistance ('impedance' is the more correct term) to the outgoing air and so there is only a very small pressure drop in the neighborhood of the glottis. As a result the pressure of the air in the mouth is much the same as the pressure below the vocal folds.

Consider the oral pressure and flow in the utterances shown in figures 3.4 and 3.5. Figure 3.4 has three records made while saying the sentence *He paid the **price***, with the emphasis on the last word. Figure 3.5 shows similar records made while saying *He **paid** the price*, with the emphasis on the second word.

The top line in each of these figures is the record produced by the microphone. It represents a rather distorted sound, as the voice was muffled by a mask. The only information it gives us is that there are four syllables, and that the third one, *the*, is the weakest. The airflow signal in the second line of each figure shows the bursts of air that occur when the lips open for each of the aspirated p^h stops. You can also see the vibrations of the vocal folds. Every time the vocal folds open the flow increases slightly. Usually these variations in flow occur so rapidly that they blur together and just form a thickening of the mean flow line.

The pressure records in the third line of each figure are chiefly remarkable for the way in which they show the increase in the pressure of the air in the mouth for each of the p^h stops. Like the flow records, they also show the variations in pressure associated with the voicing. In making these records the tip of the tube inserted between the lips must have been behind the alveolar ridge, as the record shows that the pressure in the mouth increases for **d** at end of *paid* and for **ð** in *the*.

In the sentence in figure 3.4 the oral pressure is clearly highest in the first consonant of the last word, which receives the emphasis. In the sentence in figure 3.5, when the emphasis is on *paid*, it is the p^h in this word that has the higher pressure. As the pressure in the mouth during p^h is very similar to the pressure of the air in the lungs – the driving respiratory force – we can conclude that emphatic stress in these utterances involves an increase in respiratory force

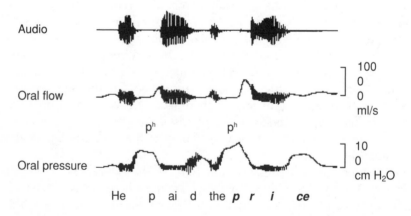

Figure 3.4 Audio, oral flow and pressure records during the sentence *He paid the price*.

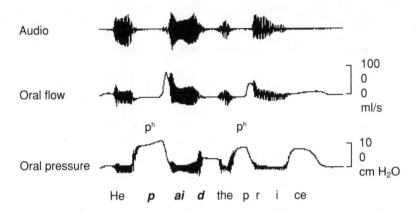

Figure 3.5   Audio, oral flow and pressure records during the sentence *He paid* the price.

(and perhaps other factors not considered here, such as an increase in glottal activity, which also causes a higher pitch).

3.2   Measuring Air Pressure and Airflow

The scales in figures 3.4 and 3.5 allow us to measure the airflow and pressure data so that we can quantify the difference between the two sentences in terms of meaningful numbers. As Lord Kelvin put it, you don't really know anything until you can express it in terms of numbers. We need to measure the airflow and pressure in several sentences, as spoken by several speakers of the dialect being investigated, and then show that the differences we are considering occur with statistical regularity in stressed syllables. Otherwise it might just be a chance difference that happened on one occasion – which is all I'm showing you here.

Flow is measured in terms of the volume of air that passes a given point in a second. We normally speak of the airflow through the lips or the nose, although we are really measuring the volume of air that passes across the mesh in the mask. The units are milliliters per second (ml/s). Voicing during conversational speech has a mean flow rate of about 250 ml/s. The bursts after an aspirated stop may be as high as 1,000 ml/s. The transducers used for measuring airflow are usually fairly stable, but you should calibrate the system at least before and

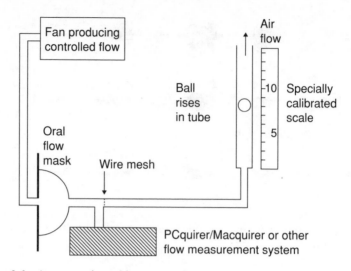

Figure 3.6   A system for calibrating airflow. As air is pushed through the mask a small pressure is built up in front of the wire mesh. This pressure is a measure of the rate of airflow.

after going out on a field trip. Calibrating the rate of flow requires the apparatus shown in figure 3.6. A fan produces a steady airstream that flows first through the mask and then on through a special flow calibration tube containing a ball that is blown higher in the tube as the flow is increased.

Pressure is measured in terms of the force required to raise or lower the height of a column of water by a certain amount. As we saw earlier, this corresponds to how much effort you would have to use to blow bubbles out of a tube immersed in water as shown in figure 3.7. This technique can be used to calibrate a pressure measurement system. In normal conversation, the force required to keep the vocal folds vibrating corresponds to holding up (or pushing down) a column of water 8 cm high. The figure shows a force being exerted to produce bubbles at the end of a tube 12.5 cm below the surface, a pressure of 12.5 cm H_2O, to use the usual abbreviation. This is about the pressure required to talk to a large group of people. Loud shouting may involve pressures of 25 cm H_2O or higher.

In a laboratory calibration measurements are usually made using a U-tube as shown in figure 3.8. When the tap is open, the tube can be filled with water to the zero level, with the water level reaching the

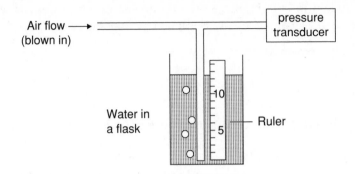

Figure 3.7   A simple system for measuring pressure.

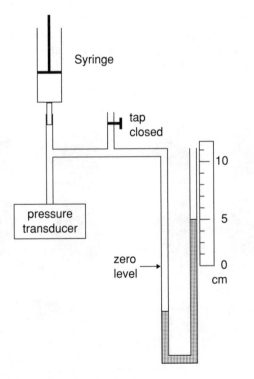

Figure 3.8   Using a U-tube to calibrate pressure.

same height in both branches. The figure shows what happens when the tap is closed and pressure is applied by pushing the syringe down. In this case the level has gone up by 5 cm on the one side and gone down by 5 cm on the other side, so that the pressure being applied is 10 cm H_2O.

3.3   Interpreting Aerodynamic Records

A large amount of information can be obtained from pressure and flow records, as we will see by looking at records of the stops that occur in Madi', a Central Sudanic language spoken in the Congo Republic. Figure 3.9 shows the pressure and airflow in (1) a voiceless and (2) a voiced bilabial stop. The speaker used a face mask to record the oral flow, and a small tube with the open end just inside his lips so as to record the pressure of the air in the mouth.

In record (1) in figure 3.9, the oral flow ceases and the pressure goes up and remains fairly level during the closure for **p**. This stop is comparatively unaspirated. The pressure falls and the flow rises so that there is a short burst, with a duration equivalent to two or three vocal fold vibrations. On another record of this utterance, using an

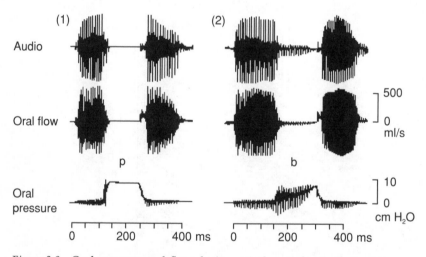

Figure 3.9   Oral pressure and flow during voiceless and voiced stops in Madi', in the words (1) **ūpà** and (2) **ūbà**.

expanded time scale, it was possible to see that the delay before the onset of voicing was 27 ms.

Record (2) in figure 3.9 shows an intervocalic **b**. The oral pressure record has strong voicing vibrations during the first part of the closure, gradually diminishing as the pressure of the air increases. There must be sufficient airflow through the glottis for the vocal folds to be kept vibrating. When the pressure of the air in the mouth has built up so that it is only slightly less than that below the vocal folds, vibrations will cease. At the end of the closure the vocal folds are in the position to vibrate, but are unable to do so as there is insufficient flow. They do not start vibrating fully until shortly after the release of the closure, which is clearly visible in the flow record.

Figure 3.10 illustrates two stops with complex articulations in Madi'. This language, like several other languages spoken in West Africa and northern Central Africa, has voiced and voiceless labial velar stops, in which the labial and velar closures are almost simultaneous. Figure 3.10 exemplifies these two sounds.

In the middle of record (3) in figure 3.10, starting at time (1) as indicated on the pressure record and ending at time (3), there is an interval in which there is no oral flow except for the two or three

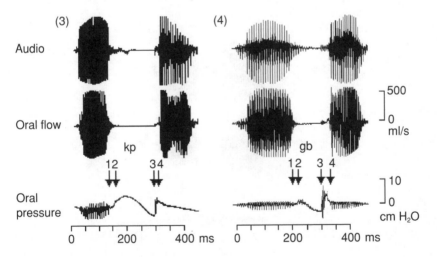

Figure 3.10   Oral pressure and flow during voiceless and voiced stops in Madi', in the words (3) **ūkpā** and (4) **'bùgbā**. Arrows indicate time points discussed in the text.

vibrations after the closure has been made. Looking at the oral pressure record, we can see that there is virtually no increase in pressure immediately after time (1), as it is the velar closure that is made first, and the open end of the oral pressure tube is in front of this closure. At time (2), the oral pressure rises because the lips have closed and the tongue and jaw are still moving upward to form the labial and velar stops, compressing the air in the space between the **k** and **p** closures. A little later the oral pressure falls as the tongue and jaw move downwards for the final vowel. By time (3) there is a negative pressure, a slight suction, in the space between the closures. This pressure rises sharply as the velar closure is released at time (3), and air passes through the glottis making the vocal folds vibrate. At time (4) the labial closure is released and the oral pressure falls. The records for the voiced labial velar stop in (4) in figure 3.10 are similar to those of the voiceless counterpart, except more voiced vibrations are visible, particularly in the interval between times (3) and (4), when there is a bilabial closure but no velar closure.

The final bilabial stop in Madi' is an implosive **ɓ**, as shown in figure 3.11. Voiced implosive sounds have a downward movement of the vibrating glottis, enlarging the vocal tract and lowering the oral pressure. However, this pressure decrease is offset by the fact that air from the lungs is flowing through the glottis, keeping the vocal folds

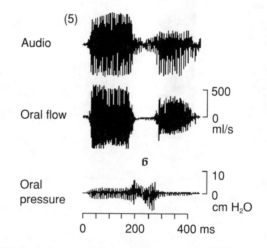

Figure 3.11   Oral pressure and flow during a voiced bilabial implosive in Madi', in the word (5) **uɓā**.

Some people get the idea of aerodynamic research very quickly. We were camping in Namibia's Etosha National Park – a wonderful place where we had chased three ostriches down a bush road and later had to stop because an enormous bull elephant was wandering around. Our task was to record the oral and pharyngeal pressure and the oral and nasal flow in clicks as spoken by groups of Bushmen. On our way out Jan Snyman, the linguist organizing our visit, said that he had heard that one of the rangers at the gate spoke Gǃui, an endangered Khoisan language. Although he would be the only speaker of the language that we could find (we normally try to record at least half a dozen people), we stopped to record him. We asked him to say a set of sounds that we could compare with the other languages we had been recording. He inserted a pressure recording tube through his nose very easily, and handled the flow masks well. After we had recorded the sounds he looked at the computer with us, pointing at places where pressure built or the nasal flow increased, fully understanding how the data helped us to describe his pronunciation.

vibrating. The oral pressure record in figure 3.11 first rises slightly and then goes below zero, before finally returning to a mean of zero when the lips open. Implosives seldom have a large negative pressure. They also differ from voiced plosives (as exemplified by (2) in figure 3.9) by having increasingly strong vibrations of the vocal folds immediately before the release of the closure.

Before we leave these five records of Madi' consonants, there is another point to be considered. In chapter 1 we noted the importance of thinking out and even starting to write the report on the sounds of a language as early as possible, long before finishing fieldwork. If you follow this practice you will know while you are still working with speakers the points you want to illustrate. Plan the figures accordingly. Think how they should look early on, and try to collect the data with that in mind. It is much easier to write the final account of a set of contrasts if you already have good pictures that make the points for you. One of the worst possible tactics when doing research is to write a description of an event, and then have to look for a possible illustration. Figures should come first, and the writing afterwards.

The next example of information that can be gained from aerodynamic data concerns voiceless nasals. In most languages that have

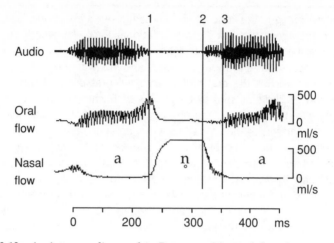

Figure 3.12   An intervocalic nasal in Burmese. (1) nasal flow begins;
(2) voicing begins; (3) nasal flow ends and oral flow begins.

voiceless nasals, they are like those in Burmese, as exemplified in figure 3.12. The oral flow increases towards the end of the first vowel as
a more breathy voice is produced. Then, at time (1), nasal flow begins.
At time (2), while there is still nasal flow but no oral flow, voicing
begins again, so that for a brief time there is a regularly voiced nasal **n**.
At time (3) the nasal flow ceases and the final voiced vowel is formed.

Angami, a Tibeto-Burman language spoken in India, has a different kind of voiceless nasal that would have been difficult to describe
without having oral and nasal flow records of the kind shown in
figure 3.13. In this language there is nasal flow during the first vowel,
which continues with fairly strong voicing for several vibrations after
the oral flow has ceased at time (1). Then at time (2), long before
voicing vibrations begin at time (3), oral flow starts abruptly. But nasal
flow still continues, although at a diminished rate, forming a kind of
nasalized aspiration in the interval between times (2) and (3). Voicing,
when it starts at time (3), is produced with considerable oral flow,
indicating that it is a breathy phonation. When listening to this sound
one gets the impression of a voiceless nasal followed by a voiceless
aspirated stop, and, indeed, this is the way the sound had been described. But the flow records make it plain that there is not a voiceless
closure immediately before the burst of airflow from the mouth, and
this sound is better described as a voiceless aspirated nasal.

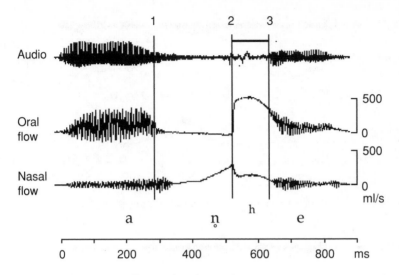

Figure 3.13 An intervocalic nasal in Angami.

3.4 Quantifying Nasalization

An oral and nasal flow system can be used to determine the extent of nasality. Figures 3.14, 3.15 and 3.16 show my pronunciation of the three phrases *Say bead again*, *Say bean again*, and *Say mean again*. In each case the vertical scale of the nasal airflow record has been expanded so that it is almost double that of the oral flow. Both flow records have also been smoothed, so as to make the mean flow more apparent. In figure 3.14,

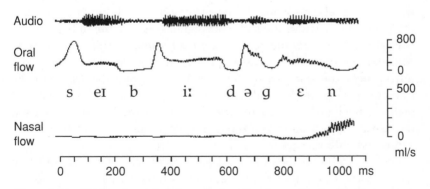

Figure 3.14 Oral and nasal airflow during the phrase *Say bead again*.

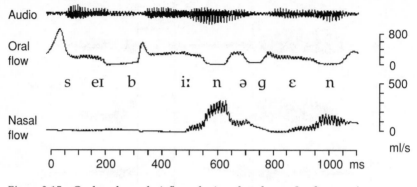

Figure 3.15   Oral and nasal airflow during the phrase *Say bean again.*

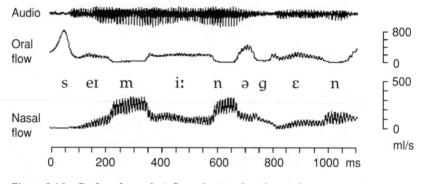

Figure 3.16   Oral and nasal airflow during the phrase *Say mean again.*

Say bead again, there is no nasal flow until the end of the phrase, during the final consonant of *again*. The oral flow shows the peaks for the releases of each of the stop consonants, and for the initial **s**.

Figure 3.15 shows the phrase *Say bean again*. In this case there is considerable nasal airflow during the final **n** of bean, and some flow during both the last part of the vowel in *bean* and the whole of the first vowel of *again*. We could quantify this by saying that the last 27% of the vowel in *bean* was nasalized, and that during that time the mean nasal flow was 13% of the total flow (a nasal flow of 40 ml/s as compared with an oral flow of 275 ml/s).

Figure 3.16 shows the phrase *Say mean again*, which has nasal airflow almost throughout after the initial **s**, even through what is labeled as the voiced stop **g** in *again*. The airflow during **m** is 220 ml/s, and during the vowel in *mean* it is 120 ml/s. This is 41% of the total air-flow, the oral airflow at that time being 175 ml/s.

3.5   Aerodynamic Investigation of Phonation Types

Pressure and flow records also provide useful data on the way the vocal folds are vibrating. In a breathy voice there is a higher rate of flow than in regular voicing (modal voice). The opposite is true in creaky or laryngealized voice, which has a very low flow rate. Of course, there will also be a higher rate of flow if the subglottal pressure is higher, but if we find the pressure is low while the flow rate is high, then we can be reasonably sure that there is a somewhat breathy voice quality. This is what happens in Javanese, as may be seen in figure 3.17. Java-nese has pairs of words such as **pipi** 'cheek' and **bibi** 'aunt'. Although these words are transcribed phonologically as if the one had **p** and the other had **b**, the difference is actually in the accompanying vowels. The consonants are virtually the same. These words could be tran-scribed (as in figure 3.17) pipi, p̤ip̤i with the same consonants and two dots below the vowels in the second word to indicate breathy voice.

The two words in figure 3.17 were each recorded in the frame di wɔtʃɔ . . . sapisan 'to be read . . . once', which is not shown in the figure. The flow record has been left uncalibrated as no provisions for flow calibration were available at the time. But it is evident that the variations in oral flow were much greater in the second word. Each vibration of the vocal folds let through a larger pulse of air than in the first word.

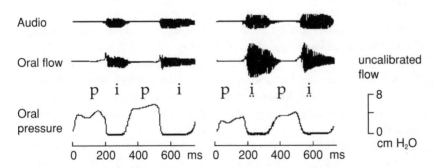

Figure 3.17   Two Javanese words, the second word being pronounced with a more breathy voice quality.

This is not because there was a higher subglottal pressure in these syllables, as the pressure in the surrounding consonants was lower in the second word. We may conclude that the second word was produced with a breathy voice quality.

3.6   Electroglottography

Another technique for investigating variations in phonation is electro-glottography (EGG), which provides a measure of the degree of closure of the vocal folds. This is not, properly speaking, an aerodynamic technique, but it is appropriate to consider it here while discussing techniques for investigating phonation types in the field. The system measures the low-voltage current between two small plates placed on the neck on either side of the larynx. When the vocal folds are together a larger current is passed than when they are coming apart. The tighter the contact the less the resistance between the plates and the larger the current.

Figure 3.18 shows the aerodynamic and laryngeal activity that occurred during the pronunciation of the Montana Salish phrase tʃʼə́tʃenʼ (phonologically tʃʼtʃenʼ) 'Where to'. The top two lines show the EGG activity, the second line showing the whole word, and the top line just a small portion of the word on an expanded time scale. The word begins with an ejective affricate, tʃʼ, during which the glottis first moves up to compress the air in the mouth, and then moves down as the ejective closure is released. When making an EGG record it is necessary to choose whether to record the fine detail of each opening and closing of the vocal folds (which was the choice made on this occasion) or the gross movements of the larynx. This record shows only that there is a great deal of glottal activity during the tʃʼ at the beginning of the word, and not a precise picture of the larynx moving up and down. Even when set to record the gross movements of the larynx, EGG records seldom show laryngeal movements in a way that can be interpreted with any reliability. They are particularly difficult to interpret when obtained from people with thick necks.

The EGG at the end of the word is more interesting. Montana Salish contrasts a so-called glottalized nʼ, written in the orthography as ʼn, and a regular, normally voiced, n. The glottalized nʼ has creaky voice vibrations of the vocal folds, which can be seen in the expanded part

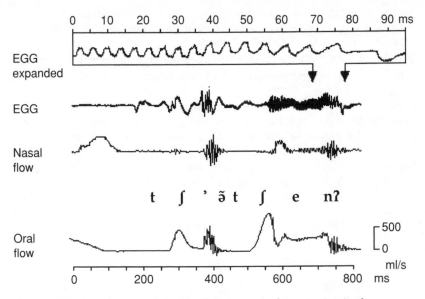

Figure 3.18 Aerodynamic records of a plosive and an ejective in the Montana Salish word **tʃˀətʃenˀ** (phonologically **tʃˀtʃenˀ**) 'Where to'.

of the EGG record in the top line. In the first part of this expanded record the waveform has a comparatively flat top when the vocal folds are apart and a similar flat base when they are together. Towards the end of this record the waveform is more triangular in shape, with the vocal folds becoming more tightly pressed together during each vibration. At the end there is a complete glottal closure.

EGG records are hard to interpret, as they do not directly relate to either movements of the larynx as a whole or the shape of the vibrating vocal folds. They simply show the electrical impedance between two plates placed on either side of the larynx. They do, however, indirectly indicate changes in the mode of vibration of the vocal folds.

3.7 Further Reading

General accounts of aerodynamic mechanisms:
Baken, R. J., and Orlikoff, R. F. (2000). *Clinical measurement of speech and voice,* (2nd edn.), chapters 8 and 9. San Diego: Singular Publishing.

Shadle, C. (1997). The aerodynamics of speech. In Hardcastle, W. J. and Laver, J. (eds.) *The handbook of phonetic sciences*. Oxford: Blackwell (Blackwell Handbooks in Linguistics, 5), pp. 33–64.

Warren, D. W. (1996) Regulation of speech aerodynamics, in Lass, N. (ed.) *Principles of experimental phonetics*. St. Louis: Mosby, pp. 46–92.

Studies demonstrating the use of aerodynamic techniques:

Dart, S. (1987). An aerodynamic study of Korean stop consonants: Measurements and modeling. *Journal of the Acoustical Society of America*, 81(1), 138–47.

Shadle, C., and Scully, C. (1995). An articulatory-acoustic-aerodynamic analysis of [s] in VCV sequences. *Journal of Phonetics*, 23, 53–66.

4

Pitch, Loudness, and Length

4.1 Pitch Analysis

Before we start discussing the analysis of pitch, we must be clear what we mean by this term. Strictly speaking, pitch is an auditory property – something you hear. It is not an acoustic property – an aspect of the sound wave that you can measure. From a practical point of view when discussing the pitch of the voice, it can usually be said to be the rate at which vocal fold pulses recur, and thus the fundamental frequency of the sound wave.

Tone and intonation are manifested by pitch. You cannot literally measure the pitch of a recorded sound, but you can measure the fundamental frequency of the sound wave, which is the acoustic correlate of pitch. The first step is to transfer the recordings to be analyzed onto a computer (a process that we will comment on further in section 4.4 and in chapter 5). Once this has been done, there are many computer programs that will make fundamental frequency

> I've never been very good at transcribing tones. I'm a fair observer of vowels and consonants, and used to be able repeat accurately whatever my language consultant said, even if it included a string of ejectives and unusual vowels. (I can no longer do this so convincingly as I'm becoming too deaf.) But, although I can mimic the tone and intonation being used, I've always found it hard to give good descriptions of subtle changes in pitch. I don't sing very well either. So good pitch extraction systems have been very helpful to me in recent years.

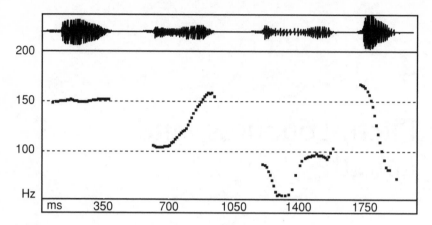

Figure 4.1   Analyses of four Chinese words **ma˥** (high level) 'mother', **ma˦**
(high rising) 'hemp', **ma˩** (low falling rising) 'horse', and **ma˥˩** (high falling)
'scold'. The top panel shows the waveform.

analyses, a process commonly referred to as pitch tracking. I will be
using the PCquirer/Macquirer system mentioned in chapter 1 in most
of the following analyses. Figure 4.1 shows an analysis of the four
Chinese tones exemplified by the words **ma˥** (high level) 'mother',
ma˦ (high rising) 'hemp', **ma˩** (low falling rising) 'horse', and **ma˥˩**
(high falling) 'scold'. The top line in the figure shows the waveforms
of these four words.

   Determining the pitch (more accurately, the fundamental frequency)
of a sound demands a lot of computation, even for a computer. Many
computer analysis systems offer a choice between a 'low resolution'
pitch analysis system that uses a computer algorithm that is comparatively rapid, and a 'high resolution' system that is slower but more
accurate. With today's more powerful computers you should always
use the more accurate analysis. There are, however, other choices that
have to be considered in order to get the best possible representation
of the pitch.

   Some of the options that have to be considered in a pitch extraction
system are shown in figure 4.2. This is part of the dialog box in the
Macquirer/PCquirer system. The computer system you are using may
not have exactly these options, but all pitch extraction programs
will (or should) provide similar choices. Over and above the choice
between Low resolution and High resolution (and, as noted above, I

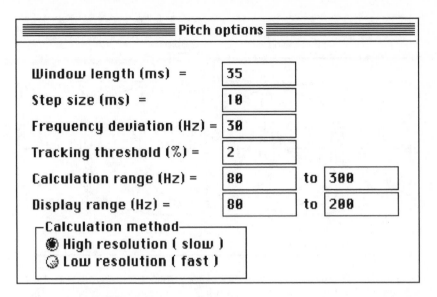

Window length (ms) = [35]

Step size (ms) = [10]

Frequency deviation (Hz) = [30]

Tracking threshold (%) = [2]

Calculation range (Hz) = [80] to [300]

Display range (Hz) = [80] to [200]

Calculation method
● High resolution (slow)
○ Low resolution (fast)

Figure 4.2   Some of the options available in a computer pitch tracking system.

would recommend always using High resolution), there are several other possibilities.

The first two points to consider are the window length and the step size. The difference between these two is best explained by looking at another view of a waveform. Figure 4.3 shows a section near the end of the third word in figure 4.1. In this very expanded view the individual pulses of the vocal folds are clearly visible.

Parts of the wave have been enclosed in slightly distorted ovals. These are so-called Hamming windows, the parts that are used in each analysis. Different programs use windows with different shapes, but small variations in window shape have been shown not to matter very much. All that is important is that the parts of the waveform near the edges are given less emphasis than the part in the center of the window. What is particularly damaging to the analysis is an abrupt change from the maximum or minimum amplitude to zero, as would have occurred at the right-hand end of the first window if a so-called square window (indicated by the dashed lines) had been used.

The window length is the duration of the piece of the waveform that the system uses in calculating the frequency. This must be long enough to include at least two cycles of the waveform. (In the

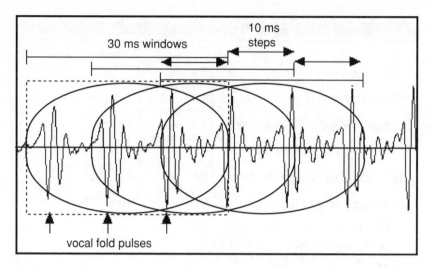

Figure 4.3   An expanded view of part of the waveform of the third word in figure 4.1. The three ovals show Hamming windows enclosing parts of the wave, and the dashed rectangle indicates a so-called square window.

waveform in figure 4.3 there are about 3 cycles in each window.) Calculating the length of a cycle involves comparing one part of the wave within the window with another part within the same window and determining that they have similar shapes. The program has to find a complete cycle before it can determine how long that cycle is.

If there is a very low pitch, the window length must be increased. Glottal pulses occurring at a rate of 50 Hz are 20 ms apart, so it would be impossible to get two cycles in a single 30 ms window. When calculating the pitch tracks in figure 4.1 the window length was increased to 50 ms so as to ensure that there would be two pulses within the window.

The step size is the amount that the window is moved over before calculating the pitch again. The default step size is 10 ms, which is fine in all descriptions of tone and intonation (though it may not be when gaining data for use in a speech synthesis system).

The next two options listed in figure 4.2 are the frequency deviation and tracking threshold. They are both concerned with tidying up the pitch curves. The rate at which the vocal folds vibrate cannot vary rapidly. If the pitch tracking system finds a pitch of, say, 100 Hz in one window, and then a pitch of 150 Hz in the next window, something must be wrong. The pitch analysis has made an error in interpreting what constitutes a vocal fold pulse. The frequency deviation option provides a way of controlling this situation. If the difference in the calculated frequency in adjacent windows is greater than the stipulated value, then it is not reported. A default value of 30 Hz is appropriate.

The tracking threshold (sometimes, in other systems, separated into the Silence threshold and the Voiced/unvoiced cost) controls the sound level at which the pitch tracking system starts operating. Using the default of 2%, no attempt will be made to report the pitch if the signal level is less than 2% above the noise level. Pitch tracking is not reliable during low-level sounds, when the individual cycles in the waveform are hard to separate from background noise. The pitch tracker might report non-existent pitch points in these circumstances.

One way of appreciating the difference these options make is by seeing what happens when they are, in effect, turned off. Figure 4.4 shows three pitch analyses of a recording of the phrase *I saw two men*. The first has the default values for these options, a permissible frequency deviation of 30 Hz and a tracking threshold of 2%. This analysis makes a few mistakes, notably in dropping one or two points in the **m** of *men*, and in failing to report a pitch as the sentence falls into creaky voice at the end.

The second analysis makes numerous errors. It has a permissible frequency deviation of 500 Hz and a tracking threshold of zero. As a result the system tries to find a pitch at every moment in time, without worrying about how the analysis of one window relates to the analysis of the previous or following windows (as long as it is within 500 Hz), and with no concern as to the level of the signal. There is a scattering of points all through the **s** in *saw*, and through much of the **t** in *two*, although there were no vocal fold vibrations in these sounds. We know the vocal folds were not vibrating at these times through our knowledge of phonetics, but of course the computer analysis system has no access to knowledge of this kind. It simply takes the wave-form and looks for a pitch at every moment. Analyses with errors that phoneticians can disregard may sometimes be useful. It may be important to record the pitch during consonants (if, for example, you are studying the effect that consonants have on tones). You can get better records by not only setting the tracking threshold to zero, but also increasing the output level of the playback when transferring the sounds onto the computer. The recording of the vowels may be distorted, but the consonants will show up better.

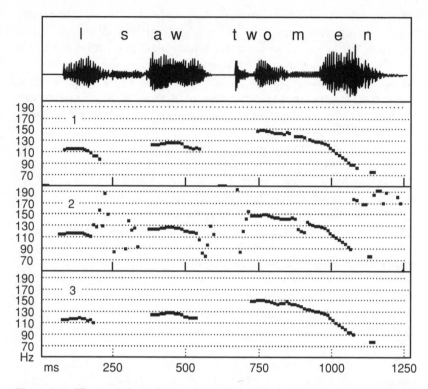

Figure 4.4 Three pitch analyses of the phrase *I saw two men*. (1) with default options for frequency deviation and tracking threshold. (2) with a frequency deviation of 500 Hz and a tracking threshold of zero. (3) with a frequency deviation of 30 Hz and a tracking threshold of zero.

The third analysis uses the best values I could find for this particular recording. It has a permissible frequency deviation of 30 Hz and a tracking threshold of zero. This is a clean recording with little background noise and it was possible to use these low values. The missing points in the **m** of *men* were recovered, but the analysis still could not find the pitch at the end of *men*, where the vocal fold vibrations change into creaky voice. The waveform (at the top of the figure) alters abruptly at this point. The amplitude of the first creaky voice pulse is about half the amplitude in the preceding series of regular glottal pulses. The pitch-finding algorithm cannot find the onset of this new pulse and loses track.

When working on tone languages, don't expect too much help from native speakers. Some of them may be able to tell whether the pitch of the voice rises or falls during a given word, but many cannot. As far as they are concerned, two words differing in tone just sound different, and they may be no more able to say how they differ than most speakers of English can tell how *head* and *hid* differ. I once went through a list of Ebira tone words that I had made with a university student in Nigeria who was a native speaker of Ebira. At one point I wondered whether a certain word had a high or a mid tone. 'Don't ask me,' he said. 'All I know is that one moment you were talking about a kind of worm, and the next asking me about dinner.'

The final options are the calculation range and the display range. The default values, 80–500 and 80–300, are appropriate for many voices, but deep bass voices (or studies involving creaky voice) will require a lower setting, say 50 Hz. (The window length will also have to be increased to 50 ms or more.) Children and some women will require higher ranges. The display range should be set to whatever makes the most appropriate picture. The PCquirer/Macquirer system does not make errors because of an unnecessarily large range, but many other pitch-tracking systems are less able to cope with a wide range of frequencies. You can estimate the range by making a preliminary analysis first and then setting both the calculation range and the display range so that they are close to what appear to be the speaker's limits.

Some pitch systems do not provide all these options. Others include a considerable amount of smoothing, eliminating minor ups and downs, and joining up points separated by small gaps, so that it is not clear that they are reporting the true pitch. How can you tell what the pitch (in the sense of the rate of repetition of the vocal fold pulses) really is? The most reliable (and the most time-consuming) way is to measure the interval in milliseconds (to the nearest tenth of a millisecond) between each vocal fold pulse, and consider the frequency to be 1,000 divided by this number. If the interval between pulses is 10 ms the rate must be 100 pulses in one second, so the pitch is 100 Hz. If two vocal fold pulses are 10.4 ms apart, the frequency at that moment is $1,000/10.4 = 96$ Hz.

Figure 4.5 shows an expanded version of the waveform of the third word in figure 4.1, the word that is most difficult to analyze correctly.

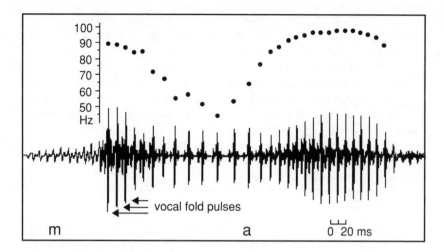

Figure 4.5   An expanded view of the waveform of the third word in figure 4.1, together with a plot of the rates at which vocal fold pulses occur.

Above the waveform there is a pitch curve that has been calculated in this way. I measured the intervals between consecutive pulses to the nearest tenth of a millisecond, using an even more expanded waveform, and was able to calculate the pitch corresponding to each pulse. This curve is very similar to the one in figure 4.1. You can see that in the part of the wave above the time scale at the lower right the vocal fold pulses are almost 10 ms apart, so the pitch is 100 Hz. In the middle of the word where the pitch is lowest, adjacent pulses are almost 20 ms apart.

Why are the automatic pitch extraction and the hand analysis different? One reason is that the computer program was set so that it could not detect vocal fold pulses that are more than 20 ms apart, making the lowest frequency it could report 50 Hz. A more important reason is that a human observer can see what constitutes a new glottal pulse more easily than a computer program can. A computer program calculates the length of a cycle by comparing one part of the wave with another and determining that they have similar shapes. It can report a pitch value only when it has found a part of a sound wave that is nearly a repetition of another part. In the creaky-voiced part of the third word being analyzed in figure 4.1 some of the waveforms produced by successive glottal pulses are very different from one

another. As a result the program, which considers the whole waveform and not just the initial spike, could not find two similar cycles,
and failed to report a pitch on two occasions in this low-frequency
part of the wave. A human can look at a waveform and note what
must be considered to be a new glottal pulse, despite the differences
in waveform. As we can see from the hand calculation in figure 4.5,
the actual lowest pitch is a little below 50 Hz. Having a fixed step size
is another reason why the pitch curves in figures 4.1 and 4.5 are different. The pitch extraction system used for figure 4.1 reports a pitch
value every 10 ms, the step size between adjacent windows used for
calculating the pitch. The hand calculation in figure 4.5 produced a
pitch point for every glottal pulse. As the glottal pulses were at varying
intervals, and always more than 10 ms apart, there are fewer points in
this curve.

Some programs follow a similar procedure to that used in the hand-
calculated pitch curve. They determine the pitch using a suitable size
window, and then, knowing the length of each pulse, locate the moment
when its onset occurs. They report the pitch only once in each pitch
period, as I did in figure 4.5. Knowing when each pulse begins is a
useful attribute for a program in that it makes it easier to re-synthesize
the speech signal with a different pulse rate, and hence a different fundamental frequency.

4.2   Interpreting Pitch Curves

Computer systems for finding pitch often make errors. The PCquirer/
Macquirer system used for this book provides very good analyses,
but many other systems are more fallible. For example the shareware
version of PCquirer/Macquirer, theWebPlayer, will sometimes provide
faulty pitch tracks, particularly of women's voices, largely because
it does not have the range of options available in the full system.
Whatever system you use, you need to watch out for possible errors,
and carefully interpret what you see. Vary the options, and see whether
the analysis can be improved. Analyzing the pitch of an utterance is
a more complicated process than it appears at first. The vocal folds do
not always vibrate smoothly and regularly. There is some art as well
as science in deciding how to represent a particular pitch curve.

When considering possible errors, the most obvious are the large
jumps that sometimes occur. One common cause of these jumps is that

two cycles can get lumped together by the analysis system so that they are considered as one. The system is looking for similarities between parts of the waveform. When it considers a sequence of four glottal pulses, the first pair may look very like the second pair. As a result the pitch will apparently be halved. This error can be avoided by preventing the pitch-tracking system from calculating too low a pitch or looking at too long a window. In the discussion of the options available, you might have wondered why the calculation range cannot be permanently set at the widest possible value. You can now see that it is advisable to limit the range so as to avoid the possibility of errors of this kind.

Another kind of error arises when a single glottal pulse gives rise to two peaks in the waveform, one when the vocal folds close and one when they come apart. This will result in one glottal pulse producing what look like two cycles in the waveform. If the pitch-tracking system finds two cycles, then the pitch reported will be double the real pitch.

As an example of the use of another pitch-tracking system, consider a pitch analysis produced by Praat. This is a program for 'doing phonetics by computer', as it says on the Praat web site at http://www.fon.hum.uva.nl/praat/. The program was developed by Paul Boersma and David Weenink of the Institute of Phonetic Sciences, University of Amsterdam. It enables users to investigate a large number of processes, from making spectrograms and pitch analyses to looking at how the ear analyzes sounds, synthesizing speech in articulatory terms, using neural nets, describing phonetic events by means of optimality theory, and much more. As a result it is more complicated and difficult to use than some other systems. But it has the great advantage of being free. You can download Macintosh or Windows versions from http://www.fon.hum.uva.nl/praat/.

Figure 4.6 shows a Praat analysis of the sounds analyzed by the Macquirer program in figure 4.1. So as to make the comparison easier, the analysis produced by the Macquirer program is shown in the lower part of the figure. Programs come and go fairly rapidly, so in making this comparison between two particular programs I may already be out of date. But similar differences between two analyses will probably always be around, as determining the pitch is a complex process that can be done in many different ways.

As is to be expected, the two analyses in figure 4.6 are very similar. The pitch tracks for the first word are almost identical. There is a

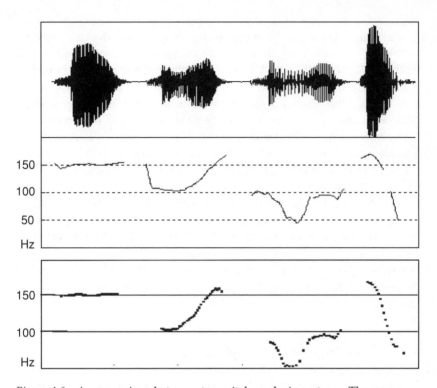

Figure 4.6   A comparison between two pitch analysis systems. The upper panel shows the waveform of the four Chinese words in figure 4.1. The middle panel is a pitch analysis produced by the Praat program, and the lower panel is the same as the analysis in figure 4.1, produced by the Macquirer program.

difference in the second word in that the Praat program suggests that this word begins with a very rapid fall in pitch. Close inspection of the waveform indicates that the first glottal pulse in this word is somewhat irregular, which the Praat program interprets as a higher pitch than the second and subsequent glottal pulses. The Praat program also does not have the slight fall that the waveform shows to occur at the end of this word. In the third word the Praat analysis is more accurate, both in showing the small variations in pitch and in showing that the pitch falls below 50 Hz. It also shows the pitch during the initial consonant. The version of the Macquirer program used for this analysis could not account for pitches below 50 Hz and could not detect the pitch in the initial consonant, which was below its intensity threshold. The greater accuracy of the Praat program in the third word causes a problem in the final word. The Praat program could not display the pitch throughout this word as it was falling at too rapid a rate. The Praat program has an option similar to the Macquirer Frequency deviation option, but if this option is set to allow for the large changes between consecutive analyses in the final word, then the analysis of the creaky voice in the third word displays numerous irregularities. The Macquirer program uses a different pitch-tracking algorithm that does not follow all the small variations in the third word, but has the complete pitch movement in the last word.

The moral of this comparison between two systems of pitch analysis is not that one is better than the other. Both of them provide generally adequate representations of the pitch, and both of them make mistakes. The point to be emphasized is that making a pitch analysis requires careful adjustment of the options. We will consider further ways of analyzing pitch in the next chapter when we discuss spectrograms.

4.3   Phonological Considerations

If we consider a perfect pitch record to be one that exactly matches each vibration of the vocal folds, there is another point to be considered. A perfect pitch-tracking system may report variations in pitch that, from a phonological point of view, may be irrelevant. So far we have been assuming that differences in tone and intonation are realized simply by the pitch. But, from a speaker's point of view, the phonetic correlate of pitch may be specific adjustments of the laryngeal muscles that control pitch. These laryngeal adjustments could be said to be what the speaker is aiming at when trying to produce a particular tone or intonation contour. The situation is complicated because the pitch of a sound is determined not only by adjustments of the laryngeal muscles, but also by the pressure drop across vocal folds and the rate of flow between them. These are factors that a speaker might not be controlling when trying to produce a certain pitch. For example, after a voiceless aspirated stop the vocal folds often begin vibrating at a higher rate because of the greater flow of air, which may sometimes be an irrelevant increase from a phonological point of view. Conversely there may be a drop in the rate of vibration during a

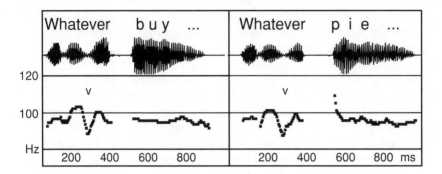

Figure 4.7   Parts of sentences beginning *Whatever buy. . . .* and *Whatever pie . . .* Note the drop in pitch during the voiced consonant **v**, and the high pitch at the beginning of the word *pie*.

voiced consonant when the flow is less, producing a lower pitch that may not be relevant.

These points are illustrated in figure 4.7. The speaker was asked to produce a series of similar sentences such as *Whatever pie you have in mind . . .* and *Whatever buy you have in mind . . .*, saying each of them with the same intonation pattern. As the parts of these sentences in figure 4.7 show, there is a considerable difference between the beginning of *buy* (which is virtually level) and the beginning of *pie* (which descends rapidly). The high pitch at the beginning of *pie* is due to the high rate of airflow for the $\mathbf{p}^h$, which continues into the beginning of the vowel, producing a higher rate of vibration of the vocal folds. Even more noticeable is the drop in each phrase for the **v** in *whatever*. The speaker's intended pitch was slightly falling from the first to the second syllable in *ever*. The major drop in pitch in between these two syllables is simply because the airflow dropped when the **v** was produced. These types of pitch perturbation are known as micro-prosody. They are usually not part of the phonology of the language, and should be disregarded in most circumstances. When we are describing the intonation or set of tones in a language we are concerned with the pitch changes that the speaker is trying to produce, and we disregard pitch changes that depend on particular segments in the words.

Small pitch variations due to changes in the rate of airflow occur fairly frequently, and often go unremarked. I did not comment on the end of the third word in the Chinese examples in figure 4.1, which rises in the last few milliseconds. This rise may well be not part of the

One of the most interesting languages that I have investigated from the point of view of stress and tone is Pirahã, a language spoken by about 300 people in the Amazonian rain forest, which may have both significant pitch (tone) and intensity (stress). I am not myself sure whether this is a correct analysis. But I am sure that the Pirahã are among the most unusual people I have ever met. They are hunter-gatherers living on the banks of the Maici river, who ignore the rest of the world and do not understand the concept of working for money. Dan Everett, who introduced me to them, tells how he once offered a Pirahã man some fish hooks if he would work with him for an hour. 'Do you fish?' the man asked. 'No,' Dan said. 'Then why don't you just *give* me the fish hooks?' the man said. 'They are no use to you.'

phonological tone but just due to an increase in the airflow as the speaker's vocal folds come apart, a common occurrence when saying lists of words.

There is another kind of pitch variation that is apt to be deceptive when studying tone. Tone languages may use intonational pitch falls to mark the end of a sentence or pitch rises to emphasize particular words. As a result, a fall in pitch marking the end of a sentence may cause a high tone to sound like a low tone. Even when simply answering a question such as 'What's your word for a frog?' a speaker may reply with an intonational fall on the last syllable. Thus the Igbo word for a frog, ówó, which actually has two high tones, may sound as if it has a high tone followed by a low tone.

Similar phonological considerations apply when analyzing pitch records with sudden jumps. It is always worth checking that a pitch analysis is valid. There is no need to make an elaborate manual analysis like the one in figure 4.5, but it is a good idea to look at an expanded version of the waveform to see whether the pulses are getting closer together where the analysis indicates that there is a rising pitch, and further apart where there appears to be a falling pitch. Whenever the analysis indicates a sudden change, examine the waveform and see why this occurs. For example, figure 4.8 is a pitch analysis of a male speaker saying the sentence *My name is Bob?* with an intonation indicating astonishment (part of a series of recordings made by Melissa Epstein when investigating voice quality changes in English). There is basically a rising pitch for the first three words and the first part of the last word. But in the middle of the last word there is a sudden

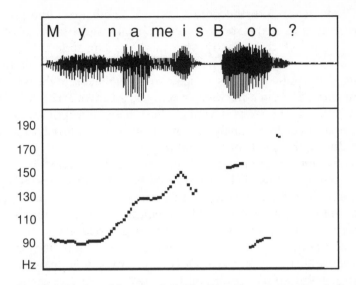

Figure 4.8 The sentence *My name is Bob?* said with an intonation indicating astonishment.

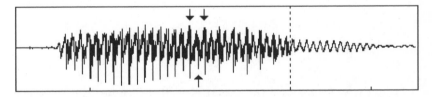

Figure 4.9 An expanded waveform of the word *Bob* in figure 4.8. The arrows are explained in the text.

drop in pitch to below 90 Hz. Is this a fault in the pitch-tracking system, perhaps a pitch halving as mentioned above, or is it real? If it is real, what should we consider the intended pitch curve to be? You can almost see the answer in the waveform above the pitch track, but figure 4.9, which shows an expanded version of the last word in figure 4.8, makes it clearer.

In the word *Bob* shown in figure 4.9 there are about 16 fairly regular vocal fold pulses before the first arrow above the waveform. After that time there is one slightly smaller pulse (marked by the arrow below the waveform), and then, from the second arrow above the waveform until the dashed line, the pulses occur at about twice the previous interval. It is as if the speaker's voice breaks and drops down into creaky voice, which is exactly what this recording sounds like. However, after the dashed line, which is when the closure for the final **b** occurred, the pulse rate goes up again to about the rate at the beginning of the word. The pitch-tracking system has given an accurate analysis of the events in this word. The pitch does change abruptly. Almost the only inadequacy in the analysis in figure 4.8 is the failure to report the pitch during the whole of the final **b**.

It is the interpretation of the abrupt change that is difficult. My first interpretation of this pitch curve would be to say that there is a pitch rise throughout the last word, and the pitch halving when the speaker moves into creaky voice is not phonologically relevant. It is a personal property of this speaker's voice, perhaps just relevant to this utterance, and not a property of the language. I don't think he was trying to produce this drop in pitch. Of course, subsequent analyses might show that this speaker dropped into creaky voice consistently, and that speakers of this dialect group also conveyed this linguistic information in the same way. Then my first interpretation would be wrong, a not uncommon event for me.

4.4   Loudness, Intensity, and Stress

The loudness of a sound can be fairly well determined by reference to its acoustic counterpart, intensity, a measure of acoustic energy. Loudness (or intensity) is sometimes considered to be indicative of stress. But stress is really not so simple to assess in instrumental terms. The auditory/acoustic consequences of a syllable having received stress in English (and in many languages) are likely to be some combination of increased pitch, length and loudness, with the first two playing the greatest roles. We have already discussed how to measure pitch, and we will consider length later in this chapter. The acoustic correlate of loudness, the third aspect of stress, is intensity, which is dependent on the amplitude of the sound wave, the size of the variation in air pressure. It is measured in decibels (dB). Roughly speaking, a change in intensity of 1 dB corresponds to the smallest change in loudness that can be heard, and a change of 5 dB corresponds to doubling the loudness. You can double the loudness of a sound many times, so that the loudest sound you can hear without being painfully deafened is about 120 dB above the faintest sound you can hear.

The intensity of a sound is measured by taking the amplitude of the waveform at each moment in time during a window, squaring it (to make it a positive number), finding the mean of all the points in the window, and then taking the square root of this mean. This is the so-called rms (root mean square) amplitude. The situation is slightly more complicated in that the intensity of one sound relative to a reference sound is calculated by comparing not the relative amplitudes but the relative powers of the two sounds. The power of a sound is the square of its amplitude. The reference sound is usually the sound with the maximum amplitude in the recording, making the sound being meas-ured so many dB below it, or the minimum level recorded, making it so many dB above it. The difference in intensity is ten times the log of the power ratio. As the power is the square of the amplitude, this is 20 times the rms voltage ratio.

Different speech sounds have different intensities, even when they have been pronounced with the same degree of stress. Other things being equal, voiced sounds have greater intensities than voiceless sounds. For vowel sounds, the intensity is largely proportional to the degree of opening of the lips. Figure 4.10 shows the waveform and loudness (more accurately, the intensity) for three phrases, *There were*

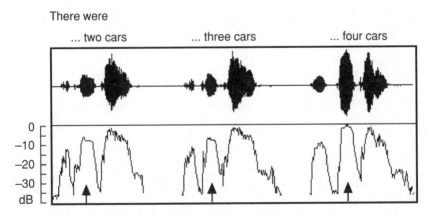

Figure 4.10   The waveforms and intensities of three phrases: *There were two cars. There were three cars. There were four cars*. The arrows are placed below the centers of the words *two, three* and *four*.

two cars, There were three cars, and *There were four cars.* Each of these phrases was said with the same stress pattern.

You can see that the first two words, *There were . . .* (spoken rapidly), and the last word, *cars,* were said with much the same intensity in all three phrases. But the words *two* and *three* have about 6 dB less intensity than *four,* in which the mouth is more open. Other things being equal, the vowel in *four* is about twice as loud as the vowels in *three* and *two.* But this does not make it any more stressed.

As a further indication that intensity is not a good indicator of stress, consider three sentences that are the same except for a contrastive stress that has been placed on a different word in each of them: *I **see** three bees* (but I can't hear them). *I see **three** bees* (not a swarm of them). *I see three **bees*** (but no wasps). In these circumstances one might expect the stressed word to have a greater intensity than the other two words that have the same vowel. But, as the pitch and intensity records in figure 4.11 show, it is mostly the pitch that indicates which word received the contrastive stress. In every case the stressed word has a higher pitch and a greater length, but not a greater intensity. A dashed line has been drawn marking the intensity of the word *see,* showing that it is almost the same in all three phrases, irrespective of whether

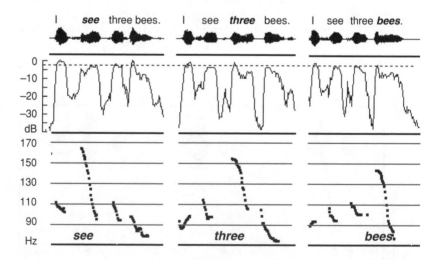

Figure 4.11 Intensity and pitch (fundamental frequency) records of *I **see** three bees* (but I can't hear them). *I see **three** bees* (not a swarm of them). *I see three **bees*** (but no wasps). The dashed line shows the mean intensity of the word *see.*

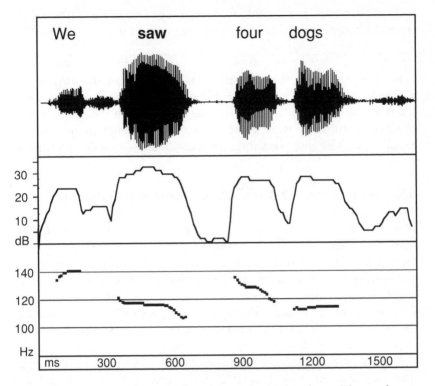

Figure 4.12   The waveform, pitch and intensity in the phrase *We **saw** four dogs*.

this word is stressed or not. The next word, *three*, has the highest intensity in the first phrase, not in the second phrase when it is stressed. Despite what you may read elsewhere (and this is why I have included this section), intensity as shown in dB is usually not a very useful acoustic property to measure. It is seldom one of the distinguishing phonetic characteristics of a language.

We should not, however, presume that an increase in pitch is always the most important correlate of stress. It is possible to emphasize words without using an increase in pitch, as exemplified in figure 4.12. This figure shows the waveform, pitch and intensity in the phrase *We **saw** four dogs*. The word *saw* has been emphasized as when denying someone who had said we could not possibly have seen four dogs. The pitch on *saw* is lower than that on *We* or *four*. The intensity is higher and the vowel is longer than usual. These last two factors, together with the fact that the pitch is very different from the pitch of the surrounding sounds (though lower rather than higher), convey the information that this is the stressed syllable.

Measuring stress from an acoustic record is difficult because the acoustic correlates of stress interact. The acoustic signal indicates that a syllable is stressed by some combination of frequency, duration and intensity (and by spectral features that we will mention at the end of chapter 7). But there is no known algorithm that enables an observer to measure these three quantities and use them as a measure of stress.

4.5   Waveforms and the Measurement of Duration

Many languages use length as a distinctive characteristic. Some languages, like Italian, have single (short) and double (long) consonants. Others, such as Finnish, have short and long vowels. In English we do not distinguish consonants or vowels by length, but both types of segment have important differences in length in different phonetic contexts. Vowel length, for example, is a significant cue to the voicing or lack of it in the final consonant in pairs of words such as *beat* vs. *bead*. Vowels are shorter before voiceless consonants than they are before the corresponding voiced consonants. Languages also differ in their use of Voice Onset Time (VOT), the interval between the release of a consonant (usually a stop) and the start of the voicing for the following vowel. Any description of the phonetic structures of a language should include an account of the VOT. In addition, if you are trying to give a full description of a language so that you can account for rhythmic differences among phrases, you will need to know the length of each segment in a variety of different circumstances.

As with investigating pitch and intensity, the first step in measuring durations is to transfer the recordings onto a computer. At this point we must consider this process more thoroughly. A sound is a continuous variation in air pressure. Storing it on a computer or a digital recorder involves turning it into a set of numbers, a process known as sampling. The sample rate is the number of numbers that represent one second of the continuous wave.

The sample rate is directly related to the frequency range that can be observed. With a sample rate of 11,000 Hz you can observe frequencies up to a theoretical limit of half the sample rate, i.e. 5,500 Hz. In practice you can properly represent somewhat less, around

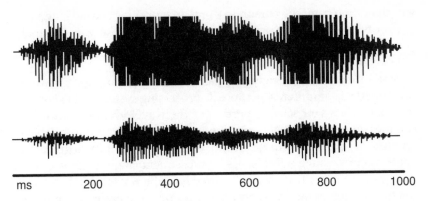

ms   200   400   600   800   1000

Figure 4.13   Two versions of the phrase *I'm going away*. The upper one is considerably overloaded.

4,500 Hz. This is sufficient for studies of vowels and voiced consonants. If you want to study fricatives or the bursts of voiceless stops, then you need to use a sample rate of 22,000 Hz, which will faithfully record frequencies theoretically up to 11,000 Hz, and practically up to about 9,000 Hz. (Sample rates around 11,000, 22,000 and 44,000 are commonly available as they are derived from the standard sample rate for an audio CD, which is 44,000 Hz.)

When recording or transferring recordings onto a computer make sure that the signal is not so high that it is overloaded. It is easy to see when this happens, as the waveform displayed on the screen appears with a flat top. Figure 4.13 shows two versions of the phrase *I'm going away*. The one in the upper part of the figure has been considerably overloaded.

When recordings are available on a computer, they can be studied in a number of ways. Computer systems will allow waveforms to be cut, copied and edited in much the same way as a written text can be manipulated by a word processor. It is often a good idea to cut out and discard irrelevant portions of a recording such as long pauses, errors, and unrelated comments. In this way you can display on the screen just the piece you are interested in, and yet the original recording is still available if needed. (If the recording was made directly onto the computer, never edit the original; always work with a copy.)

The length of the piece that is displayed on the screen can be easily varied. Most computer systems allow you to zoom in and see expanded versions. Some of them allow you to zoom in for a given length of time from the cursor, say one, two or three seconds, depending on what is being measured. Using this technique you can make sure that the window length is always the same, a great advantage when comparing a number of different waveforms.

When there is a sufficiently expanded display, duration is easy to measure on a computer. Most speech-processing systems will show the duration when you select a portion of the waveform. But before you can measure the length of any section of speech, you need to be able to identify the segments. In general it is easiest to identify segments in spectrograms, as we will discuss in subsequent chapters. However, if it is possible to identify a segment directly in the waveform, then selecting this portion of the waveform is a good way to measure its duration. For reference purposes, figure 4.14 shows a number of English consonants before the vowel **aɪ** as in *buy*, all of them at the beginning of stressed monosyllables. (If you want to listen to these particular sounds, you can find them as examples of English consonants on the web site *http://hctv.humnet.ucla.edu/departments/linguistics/VowelsandConsonants/vowels/chapter6/soundsvowels.html.*)

Look at the top row of figure 4.14, which shows a set of voiceless stop consonants. The flat line in each waveform is the closure. It is followed by irregular perturbations corresponding to the burst of noise that occurs when the stop closure is released. There are then small variations making an irregular line during the aspiration. The repetitive spikes at the end of each panel are the glottal pulses, each of which produces a complex waveform during the vowel. These features are seen most easily in **t** and **k**; **p** often has only a very small, hardly noticeable, burst, marked in this picture by an arrow.

The VOT (Voice Onset Time) is marked in the final panel in the top row. This is the interval between the burst (the first arrow in this panel) and the onset of vocal fold vibrations (the second arrow). Similar arrows could have been shown in the **p** and **k** panels, but they were omitted so that the parts of the waveform could be labeled more clearly.

The so-called voiced stops in the second row are remarkable because they have absolutely no voicing during the closure, which is a completely flat line. This is typical of English **b**, **d**, **g** when they are at the beginning of a syllable that is not preceded by a voiced sound. These stops are usually fully voiced only when they are between voiced sounds such as vowels. They are similar to the voiceless stops in the top row in that the burst is most evident for the alveolar stop, **d**, and the longest gap before voicing starts is after the velar stop, **g**.

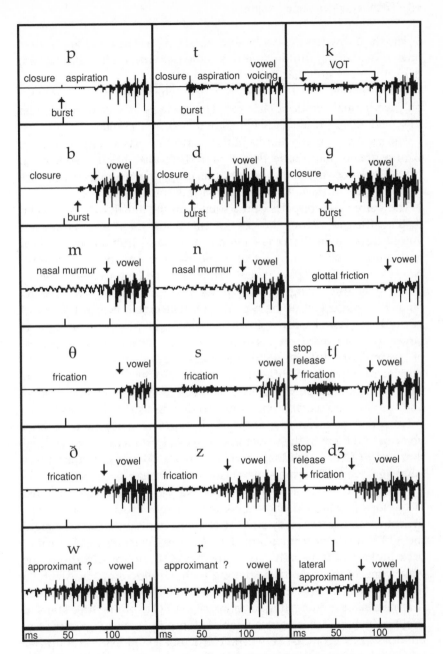

Figure 4.14 The waveforms of a number of English consonants in stressed word-initial position. The arrows indicate possible segmentation points. Queries show where there is no defined segmentation point.

The third row has the two voiced nasals, **m, n**. The vocal fold pulses have a smaller amplitude than the following vowel. The velar nasal **ŋ** does not occur in initial position in English, but its waveform is very similar. Also shown in the third row is **h**, which has a waveform with only very small random changes. The same is true of **θ** in the next row, and also of **f**, which is not shown as it is so similar.

The fricative **s**, in the middle of the fourth row, has a noisy waveform with a greater amplitude than **θ** or **f**. The other English sibilant, **ʃ**, would look very much the same as **s**, as is apparent from its occurrence as part of the affricate **tʃ** at the end of this row.

The voiced counterparts of the sounds in the fourth row are shown in the fifth row. As in the case of the stops, these sounds are not voiced throughout. There is a period of voiceless friction before vocal fold pulses start. In the case of **z** and **dʒ** it is possible to see noisy waveforms containing both vocal fold pulses and high-frequency noise.

The final row in figure 4.14 shows the approximants **w, r, l**. As far as the appearance of the waveform is concerned, **w** is just a way of beginning a vowel with a slowly increasing amplitude. The same is largely true of **r**, and would also be typical of **j**, not shown here because of its similarity. It is impossible to mark the ends of these segments. The lateral **l** is a little different in that it is often marked by a clear increase in amplitude when the vowel begins. When **r** or **l** occur after a vowel they are usually impossible to distinguish in the waveform.

Now that you can identify various types of consonants so that you can find them in the waveform, you can start measuring the duration and VOT of individual sounds. When making a description of a language, the VOT of the stop consonants should always be given, as it varies considerably across languages. Navajo has voiceless aspirated velar stops with a VOT of over 150 ms, whereas the comparable stops in Scottish Gaelic have a mean VOT of about 75 ms. In many languages the VOT increases from **p** and **t** to **k**. Stops that are made further back in the mouth usually have a longer VOT. Figure 4.15 shows the waveforms of three words beginning with voiceless stops in Aleut, an Eskimo–Aleut language spoken in the Pribilof and Aleutian islands near Alaska. It is interesting to compare the VOTs of the three stops in Aleut, which does not have a bilabial stop **p** in its native vocabulary, but does have a contrast between velar **k** and a stop made still further back in the mouth, the uvular **q**. Will **q** have a longer VOT? It looks like it from the waveforms in figure 4.15, but the scale is too small to make accurate measurements.

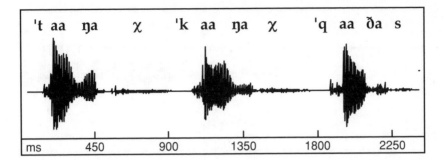

Figure 4.15   The waveforms of the Aleut words **'taaŋaχ** 'water', **'kaaŋuχ** 'healthy', and **'qaaðas** 'dolly varden' (a fish).

Most systems for displaying waveforms allow you to expand the scale considerably. Figure 4.16 shows, on a very expanded scale, the stops at the beginnings of these three words. When measuring the duration of speech sounds you should always use an expanded time scale of this kind. Each word has been lined up so that the first glottal pulse is at the dashed line below the arrow. But has this been done correctly? It is clearly correct for the **k** and the **q**, but the location of the first glottal pulse after **t** in the top panel is not so obvious. If the arrow marks a glottal pulse and not just part of the aspiration, then it is a rather feeble, breathy, pulse, with less than half the amplitude of the following pulse. The only thing to do in a case like this is to make up your mind how big an amplitude a glottal pulse should have, and what its waveform should look like, and then apply these standards to all the waves you are measuring. There are no easy answers, but one should always be consistent in one's judgments.

Next, in order to measure the VOT, the release of the articulation must be determined. The release burst is fairly clear in all three wave-forms, but this is often not the case. The release of a bilabial **p** closure is often faint and scarcely distinguishable from the background noise. Fortunately we do not have that problem in Aleut, which does not have **p**. In the Aleut sounds in these particular recordings, **t** has a shorter VOT than **k**, and **q** has the longest VOT, supporting the notion that the further back in the mouth a closure is made, the longer the VOT. However, as we noted in chapter 1, it is foolhardy to come to a conclusion about what a language does on the basis of data from one speaker, and even worse to consider only one token of each type of

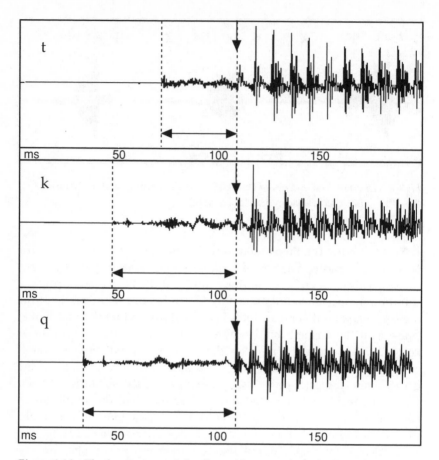

Figure 4.16   The beginnings of the three Aleut words in figure 4.15 on an expanded time scale. The downward-pointing arrows show the probable onset of regular vocal fold vibrations, and the horizontal arrows delineate the VOT.

stop. It turns out that when one considers data from 10 speakers of Aleut there is only a statistically non-significant tendency for uvular stops to have a longer VOT than velar stops.

There are many other kinds of phonetic investigation that require the measurement of the lengths of segments. For example, if we want to get good text-to-speech synthesis, we need to know how segment lengths vary in different phonetic contexts. It might be a bit far-fetched at the moment to talk about speech synthesis for languages such as

> Recording Aleut had its difficult aspects. The Aleutian people, being Native Americans, are allowed to kill sea lions, and one evening we were given raw sea lion liver for dinner. Next day, when we were about to get it again, I reminded them that the law allowed them to kill sea lions solely for their own consumption, and not for mine.

Aleut, so we will consider what has to be done for a better-known language like English. For good speech synthesis we need to know, for example, whether there is a difference in the length of initial and final consonants. With this in mind we will compare the nasals at the beginning and end of the English word *none*. The top panel of figure 4.17 shows the whole phrase *Say none today*. The first step is to check that we can identify the segments in this phrase, so that we know which parts of the waveform to expand. It is possible to distinguish the segments even in the relatively unexpanded waveform in the top panel. The initial **s** is distinct from the following vowel, the two **n**'s in *none* have a lower intensity than the vowel between them, the **t**[h] of *today* has a silent section followed by a burst of noise, the short first vowel of *today* is followed by a closure for the **d** and the longer final vowel.

For accurate measurements of the two **n** sounds we need to expand the waveforms in the sections marked (a) and (b) in the upper panel. These expanded waveforms are shown in the middle and lower parts of the figure. Looking at these portions, note that the beginning and end of the first **n** are well delineated at times (1) and (2) in the middle panel. As we have seen, nasal sounds typically have a simpler looking waveform than vowels, as most of the energy is in the lower frequencies close to the fundamental. They do not have the variations associated with higher frequencies that can be seen in each glottal pulse of a vocalic waveform. The beginning of the final **n** is well delineated in the lower panel at time (3). I have marked it as beginning in the middle of a glottal pulse, where the complexities of the vowel waveform are lost and the simpler waveform of **n** begins. But the end of this **n** is not so clear. It should probably be considered to be at the time of arrow (4), and the faint variations in waveform around arrow (5) considered to be voicing during the first part of the **t** closure. But this is by no means certain. Again, when making sets of data of this kind, what matters most is to make the measurements the same way every time, and to make a note of what you did so that you'll be able to replicate it.

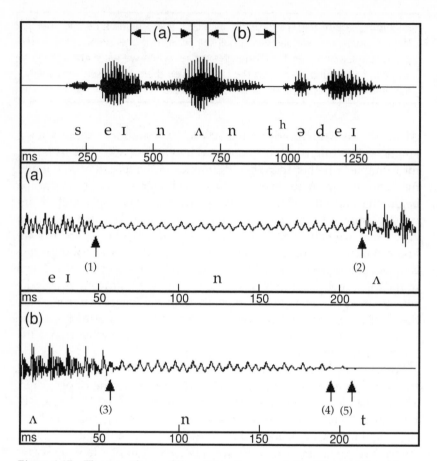

Figure 4.17 The waveform of the phrase *Say none today*. The middle and lower parts show expanded views of the portions marked off by arrows in the upper part. The numbered arrows are referred to in the text.

Are the lengths of initial and final nasals different? This is a much more complicated question than we can explore here. The lengths of segments depend on their position in the word, their position in the phrase and the whole utterance, where the stresses occur in the utterance, and many other factors. Here our only concern is *how* to measure segment length. Almost any speech analysis package will provide the numbers – the durations in milliseconds of a highlighted section of a waveform, or one bounded by two markers.

As you will gather from a number of tentative remarks in the preceding paragraphs, measuring the durations of segments in a waveform is not a straightforward task. Some books may give you the impression that it is easier to use other acoustic analysis techniques, notably sound spectrograms, which we will consider in the next chapter, but I don't think this is correct. Spectrograms cannot give such precise information in the time domain as expanded time scale waveforms, which readily permit measurements in milliseconds. It is a good idea to use spectrograms in conjunction with waveforms when making measurements, as spectrograms provide by far the better way of identifying segments. But the actual measurement of durations should be made on an expanded waveform. Even when using spectrograms in conjunction with waveforms there will be problems, as many segments do not have clear beginnings and ends. There are hard decisions to be made whatever the form of the acoustic analysis. All that one can do is choose consistent measurement points, and report the duration of each sound in the same way.

4.6   Further Reading

This is the first of a series of chapters on acoustic phonetic issues. The most comprehensive book on acoustic phonetics is:
Stevens, K. N. (2000). *Acoustic phonetics*. Cambridge, Mass.: MIT Press.

More elementary accounts include:
Fujimura, O., and Erickson, D. (1999) Acoustic phonetics. In Hardcastle, W. J., and Laver, J. (eds.) *The handbook of phonetic sciences*. Oxford: Blackwell (Blackwell Handbooks in Linguistics, 5).
Johnson, K. (2003) *Acoustic and auditory phonetics*, 2nd edn. Oxford: Blackwell.
Ladefoged, P. (1996) *Elements of acoustic phonetics*, 2nd edn. Chicago: University of Chicago Press.

5

Characterizing Vowels

The best way of describing vowels is not in terms of the articulations involved, but in terms of their acoustic properties. Introductory accounts of the acoustics of speech can be found in several texts on general phonetics, as well as in more specialized books such as those mentioned at the end of the preceding chapter. These books note that the most important acoustic properties of vowels are the formants, which can be readily seen in sound spectrograms. But the textbooks do not usually tell you how to make good spectrograms, and how to analyze and present data on the acoustics of vowels. These are the topics of the current chapter.

5.1 Sound Spectrograms

Let's assume that you want to describe the vowels of a given language, and have recorded sets of words as suggested in chapter 1. The first step is to make spectrograms of this material, so that you can get a general impression of where the formants are. Before making any measurements you need to look at spectrograms of a complete set of vowels so that you can see whether some of the vowels are diphthongs, and where in each vowel it would be best to measure. In short monosyllables such as *bead, bid, bed, bad . . .* that do not have diphthongs, an interval near the middle of the vowel is usually appropriate. If the vowel is a noticeable diphthong you should measure the formants at two points, one near the beginning,

My life was literally saved by an old-fashioned spectrograph, a large piece of hardware. I was in the Phonetics Laboratory of the University of Ibadan in Nigeria, working with an Urhobo speaker. The ceiling had been covered with soundproofing material attached to a network of 2″ × 6″ mahogany beams. Suddenly this whole false ceiling crashed down on our heads. It had been improperly fastened to the main building above. Fortunately the major part of the impact was taken by the Sound Spectrograph, which was the highest object in the room. My head, which was the next highest, took a hard hit. The Urhobo speaker sitting a little to one side felt the rest. He ended up on the floor saying 'Sorry, sir, sorry', as if it were all his fault. Fortunately I knew that, in Nigerian English, 'Sorry' was an expression of sympathy, not of guilt.

but not so close as to be part of the consonant transition, and the other near the end, but again sufficiently far from any consonantal effects.

Usually vowels can be quite well characterized in terms of the frequencies of just the first and second formants, but the third formant should also be measured for high front vowels and for r-colored vowels. Ideally you want to make measurements at a time when all three formants, or at least the first two, are comparatively steady. Unfortunately it very often happens that the most steady-state time of the first formant is not the best time for measuring the second formant, and this means that there is no simple way of defining the interval that best characterizes vowel quality. You need to look at all the data and choose a time that allows you to make consistent measurements of everything. Write down the procedures you are using to select the point for measurement, as otherwise when you come back to make another set of measurements a few weeks later, you may not be able to repeat the same procedures. Spend some time looking at the data before you begin making any measurements. It will save the problems that arise when you find that you cannot make consistent measurements because one type of vowel cannot be measured at the times you have chosen for all the rest.

In chapter 4 we discussed points to consider in transferring sounds onto a computer. Now we must consider the options for making suitable spectrograms for looking at the formants of these sounds. Figure 5.1 shows the possibilities in the Macquirer/PCquirer system. Other analysis systems will have similar options.

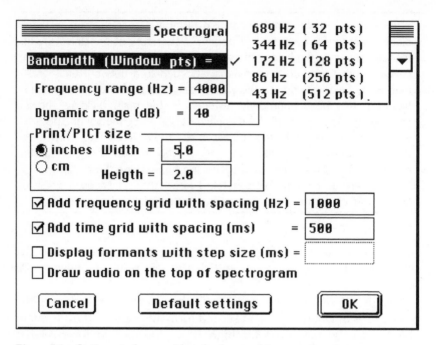

Figure 5.1   Options to be considered when making spectrograms.

The first point to be considered is highlighted at the top of the figure, the bandwidth or window length. Figure 5.2 shows the effect of varying the bandwidth when investigating the pronunciation of the vowel in *head* as spoken by a male and a female speaker. A bandwidth of around 300 Hz is sometimes called a wideband spectrogram. The left-hand spectrogram in each row in figure 5.2 is a wideband spectrogram with a bandwidth of 344 Hz. (The particular numbers used in an analysis are dependent on the sampling rate. The mathematical procedure requires the number of points in the analysis window to be a power of 2 (32, 64, 128, 256, etc.). The bandwidth is the result of dividing the sampling rate by the number of points in the analysis window. Thus 344 is 22,000/64.) In these spectrograms the first four formants of the male speaker and the first three formants of the female speaker appear as broad bands. A bandwidth of 43 Hz (=22,000/512), the right-hand spectrogram for the male speaker, produces a narrowband spectrogram, in which the individual harmonics within each formant are apparent. For the female speaker the harmonics are apparent when the bandwidth is 86 Hz (=22,000/256).

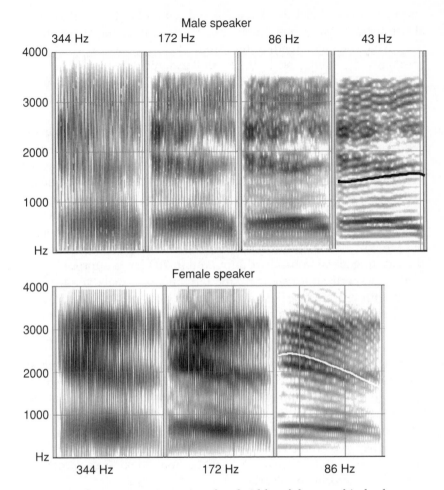

Figure 5.2 Spectrograms at various bandwidths of the vowel in *head* as spoken by a male and a female speaker. On the narrowband spectrograms on the right the tenth harmonic has been marked by a black line for the male speaker and by a white line for the female speaker.

In the preceding chapter, when discussing ways of analyzing pitch, we noted the possibility of using spectrograms. We can now see that narrowband spectrograms showing the individual harmonics provide very good information on the pitch. You can see that all the harmonics rise for the male speaker in figure 5.2. It is difficult to see the exact amount of the rise in the fundamental frequency, but the tenth harmonic, which has been marked with a black line, rises from about 1,400 Hz to around 1,600 Hz, so the fundamental frequency must have risen by a tenth of this, from 140 Hz to 160 Hz. The female speaker had a falling pitch, the tenth harmonic (most easily seen by marking with a white line in this case) going from about 2,300 Hz to around 1,600 Hz, so we can say that the pitch fell from 230 Hz to 160 Hz.

The best pictures for observing formants are those in which the bandwidth is just wide enough not to show the individual harmonics. The hardware systems for analyzing speech in the last century provided a choice of two bandwidths, 45 Hz and 300 Hz. There is still a tendency to assume that a 300 Hz bandwidth ('wide band') is the most appropriate value for looking at formants, and 45 Hz bandwidth ('narrow band') is best for looking at displays showing individual harmonics. But we now have a wider range of possibilities and can make better choices. In general, a bandwidth of around 200 Hz is appropriate for making a spectrogram showing the formants of a male voice, and a bandwidth nearer 300 Hz would be better for most female speakers. Children's voices require even larger bandwidths. The 172 Hz bandwidth in figure 5.2 is fine for the male speaker, and is probably the best for the female speaker, although in her case the individual harmonics become apparent towards the end of the vowel. Without considering both the 172 Hz and the 344 Hz bandwidth spectrograms you might get a false impression of the formant movements in the case of the female speaker. Even small changes in fundamental frequency affect the appearance of the formants. If there are large changes, as occur when recording some tone languages or emotional forms of speech, it may not be possible to make good-looking spectrograms that show the formants clearly.

To get some experience in locating formants, you might like to make a copy of figure 5.2 and try to draw a line through the centers of each of the first three formants in the spectrograms with 172 Hz bandwidths. We will see later that a computer program can do this fairly well, but it makes occasional mistakes.

The time resolution of a spectrogram depends on the bandwidth. Roughly speaking, a bandwidth of 200 Hz will separate out events that are 1/200 seconds apart, and a bandwidth of 50 Hz will separate out those that are 1/50 seconds apart. Vocal fold vibrations that have a frequency of 200 Hz or below (and thus are at least 1/200 seconds apart) will be distinguished on a spectrogram with a 200 Hz bandwidth.

After I had given a talk in one university in India one of the students asked a question about the formants of the vowels in his own language. 'That's easy to see,' I answered. 'Let's make a spectrogram.' I had noticed an old-fashioned spectrograph in a cabinet with glass doors. But I shouldn't have rushed in with so much enthusiasm. It turned out that nobody could use the spectrograph without its keeper, the senior technician, being present. He was eventually found and came in like an elderly butler in a British movie. No one had used the spectrograph for many months, and the rubber driving wheel had become so warped that it thumped as it turned in its efforts to record. I was embarrassed and wished I had found out beforehand whether the machine really worked, thus preventing a loss of face, a terrible thing in India.

If the bandwidth is only 50 Hz, the analysis will be more precise in the frequencies it shows, separating out the individual harmonics (as long as the pitch is above 50 Hz), but not showing the precise time of occurrence of each vocal fold vibration.

The other number shown in the first option is the window length, which is measured in terms of the number of points used in calculating each piece of the spectrum. As we have seen, when we want to alter the bandwidth we are in effect changing this number.

The next two options shown in figure 5.1 are the frequency range and the dynamic range. For a male speaker 4,000 Hz is an appropriate frequency range for looking at formants. Female speakers may require a range of 5,000 Hz to show the higher formants. The dynamic range, in dB, affects the range of contrasts that are shown in the picture, as shown in figure 5.3. A dynamic range of 40 dB is suitable for most purposes, but the formants often show up better if the range is reduced to 30 dB. A range of 50 dB often makes the background too dark.

The spectrograms in figure 5.3 show a male speaker of American English saying the word *dad*. The first formant is fairly constant throughout the main part of the vowel, but the second formant has a marked shift. This vowel is plainly a diphthong, and would be best characterized by noting the formants at two points, say at 120 ms and 300 ms.

The remaining options in figure 5.1 are concerned with adding frequency and time scales, and with the possibility of displaying formant tracks with a certain step size, which we will consider later.

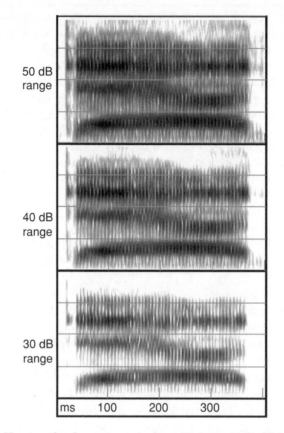

Figure 5.3 Varying the dynamic range from 50 down to 30 dB in a
spectrogram of a male speaker saying *dad*.

There are two other points we should note before leaving the topic
of making spectrograms. The first is that spectrograms usually have a
boost to the intensity of the higher frequencies, so that the appearance
of equally dark bars at different frequencies does not mean that there
is equal energy at these frequencies. Figure 5.4 shows what happens
when a series of waves at different frequencies but all with the same
amplitude are displayed. The waveform is shown at the top of the
picture, but because of the compressed time scale, separate vibrations can be seen only in the case of the lowest frequency, 50 Hz. It is
apparent that all the waves have the same amplitude. However, on the

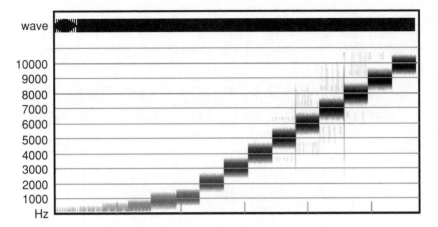

Figure 5.4   A spectrogram of a set of waves of equal amplitudes with frequencies of 50, 100, 200, 400, 800, 1,000 Hz, and then every 1,000 Hz up to 10,000 Hz. The wave itself is shown at the top.

spectrogram, the very low frequencies are hardly visible. The bars representing the different frequencies get darker as the frequency increases.

The final point concerns the vertical lines that can be seen in wideband spectrograms. Each opening and closing of the vocal folds produces a glottal pulse, a burst of sound, that appears as a vertical line. But any picture on a computer screen or produced by a computer printer also consists of closely spaced vertical (and horizontal) lines. Sometimes the distance between the vertical lines due to the vocal fold pulses is closely related to the number of vertical lines being drawn by the program. As a result there is an interference pattern, with some groups of vocal fold pulse lines becoming darker than others, as is demonstrated in figure 5.5.

Figure 5.5 shows seven spectrograms of exactly the same sound. The spectrograms differ only in their width, the number of pixels allocated to each glottal pulse on the screen and in the printout. The spectrogram at the top shows the full details of the sound, each glottal pulse being clearly shown. The spectrogram in the second row gives the impression that the glottal pulses are somewhat irregularly spaced. In the spectrograms in the third row, especially at the beginning of the one on the left and at the end of the one on the right, the vocal fold pulses appear to come in clumps. The first spectrogram in the last row

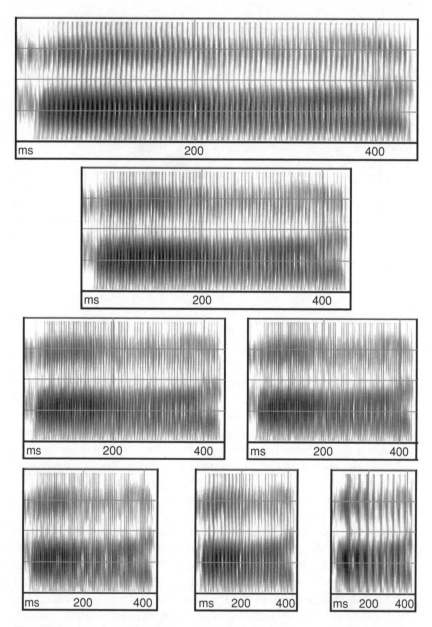

Figure 5.5   A spectrogram of the same waveform (the vowel in *hod* as said by a female speaker) at various degrees of compression of the time scale.

Once, Jenny and I were working in Thailand with a group of monks who spoke Bruu, a language with interesting vowels, some with creaky voice. Our difficulties were compounded by the fact that they were not allowed to take anything directly from a woman. Jenny had to pass me a pen so that I could hand it to a monk who wanted to write down his address. He was asking me to send him some novels in English – preferably detective stories.

continues this trend, but in the middle spectrogram something else happens; the pitch appears to be more than halved. There appear to be twelve evenly spaced pulses before the 200 ms time marker, as opposed to 31 pulses in the same interval in the spectrogram at the top of the figure. Finally, in the last spectrogram, there appear to be only nine pulses in this vowel, as if it were in creaky voice. But for all these spectrograms the sound was actually the same, with regular vocal fold pulses shown in the top spectrogram.

This phenomenon is an inevitable result of the way in which spectrograms are computed and displayed or printed. It is really troublesome only in sounds with a comparatively steady-state fundamental frequency. In these circumstances you should be especially cautious when interpreting clumps of vocal fold pulses apparently increasing and decreasing in amplitude. There may not really be any such variation in the action of the vocal folds themselves. If the variations in amplitude disappear when the time resolution is increased, then they are only an artifact of the display. But they may be real. Figure 5.6 shows a spectrogram and above it a waveform. The right-hand half of the spectrogram looks much like the last spectrogram in figure 5.5. But, as the wave at the top indicates, what actually happened was that there was a fall in pitch as the speaker uses a somewhat irregular creaky voice during the last part of the word.

Good spectrograms are a great help in determining where the formants are. This is often not as easy one might imagine. You have to know where to look for formants before you can find them. The best practical technique is to look for one formant for every 1,000 Hz. The vowel ə, for example, has formants at about 500, 1,500 and 2,500 Hz for a male speaker (all slightly higher for a female speaker). Other vowels will have formants up or down from this mid range. But there are exceptions to this general rule of one formant per 1,000 Hz. It would be more true to say that there is, on average, one formant for

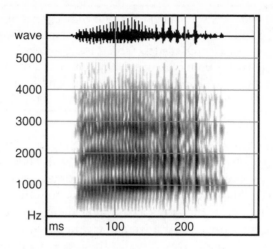

Figure 5.6   The waveform and spectrogram of the word *bat* in which the speaker uses a creaky voice during the last part of the word.

every 1,000 Hz. Low back vowels may have two formants below 1,000 Hz, but nothing between 1,000 and 2,000 Hz, and then the third formant somewhere between 2,000 and 3,000 Hz. If you know you are analyzing a low back vowel, don't be surprised to find one thick bar on the spectrogram that really corresponds to two formants close together below 1,000 Hz. Figure 5.7 is a spectrogram of my pronunciation of the word *caught*, in which the first two formants are very close together. In this spectrogram, if there are three formants below 3,000 Hz, then there must be two formants below 1,000 Hz.

Sometimes it is not immediately obvious whether a particularly wide band represents one formant or two. Figure 5.8 is a spectrogram of the word *bud*, spoken by a female speaker of Californian English. There is a wide band below 1,000 Hz, but is this one formant or two formants close together as in figure 5.7? Noting that there is a clear formant at about 1,500 Hz in figure 5.8, and additional formants higher, we must take it that there is only a single formant below 1,000 Hz. It seems that there is some kind of extra formant near the first formant, making this dark bar wider. From the evidence of this one vowel it is impossible to say whether the additional energy is above or below the first formant. Further analysis of this speaker's voice showed that there was often energy around the 1,000 Hz region, irrespective of the vowel. This spurious formant is not connected with the vowel quality,

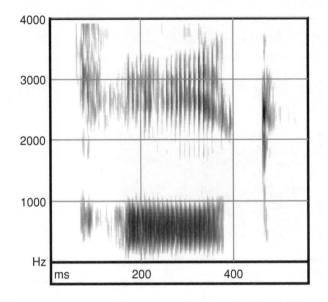

Figure 5.7   A spectrogram of the word *caught* in which the first two formants are very close together.

but is simply a characteristic of the particular speaker's voice. This is a good example of the necessity of looking at a representative sample of a speaker's voice before making any measurements of the formants.

You can get some help in locating formants by displaying the formant tracks as determined by the computer (the second-to-last option in figure 5.1). The computer finds the formants by looking for the peaks in the spectra, as we will discuss in the next section. Figure 5.9 shows a spectrogram of a set of Assamese vowels that are particularly interesting because the last vowel has the tongue position of the vowel in English *pot* but virtually maximum rounding of the lips, a vowel sound that I have not heard in any other language.

The formant tracker finds the correct formants for the first two vowels, but in the third vowel it tracks an extra formant between formants one and two. There is some energy in this region, but, if we know that this vowel sounds like ɛ, then we must consider this a spurious formant. Looking at the spectrogram it is clear that it is not a well-defined dark bar like the other formants. In the next vowel, **a**, there are some errors in the second formant. In the remaining vowels the formant tracker does quite well, especially in finding a third formant

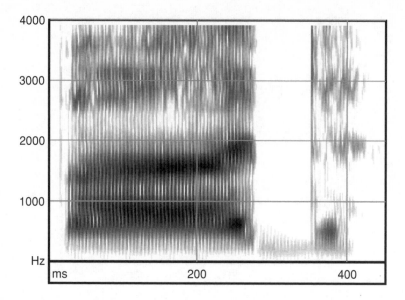

Figure 5.8   A spectrogram of the word *bud*, spoken by a female speaker of Californian English.

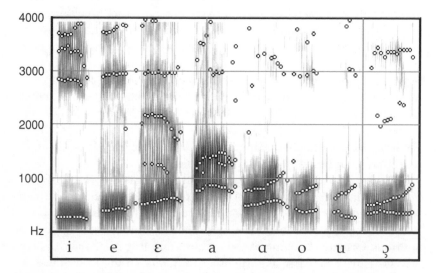

Figure 5.9   A spectrogram of a set of Assamese vowels in syllables of the form **p_t**, with added formant tracking denoted by small white circles.

I recorded these Assamese vowels at the All India Institute of Speech and Hearing at Mysore, in South India, a long way from the North East corner of India where Assamese is spoken. I was on my way to work on a completely different language, Toda, but I always try to pay my respects at local universities, in return for the privilege of working on languages in their neighborhood. I did not expect to find much at this institute, as the only day I could go was India's Independence Day, a holiday like July 4th in the USA. But I was welcomed by many students, all doing interesting advanced work in acoustic phonetics. One of them told me about the vowel system in his language, Assamese. I've learned a lot through talking to phoneticians all over the world.

that is very difficult to see. I would, however, distrust its determination of the fourth formant in most of these vowels.

Some formant-tracking systems have an option that allows you to set a minimum value of the formant amplitude required for the formant track to be shown. As we will see in the next section, formants with low amplitudes have large bandwidths. If a formant tracker finds a formant with a bandwidth greater than 400 Hz, it will have a low amplitude, and that part of the formant track should be omitted.

5.2   Spectra

Formant trackers are not the only ways to measure the formants in a vowel. The crudest, and not the best for anything except a quick assessment, is to use the cursor to make measurements directly on the spectrogram. A better technique is to calculate and display the spectrum, the amplitude of each of the component frequencies at a given moment in time. The spectrum can be calculated in a number of different ways, each giving a slightly different impression of the locations of the formants. Figure 5.10 is a typical menu showing the possibilities in this respect.

The first choice to be made is the analysis bandwidth. If you want to know fairly precisely what frequencies are present, you have to examine a comparatively long section of the sound wave. This is the same kind of choice as we discussed when considering the options for spectrograms, shown in figure 5.1. The spectrum on the left of figure 5.11 was made using a bandwidth of 344 Hz. It uses only

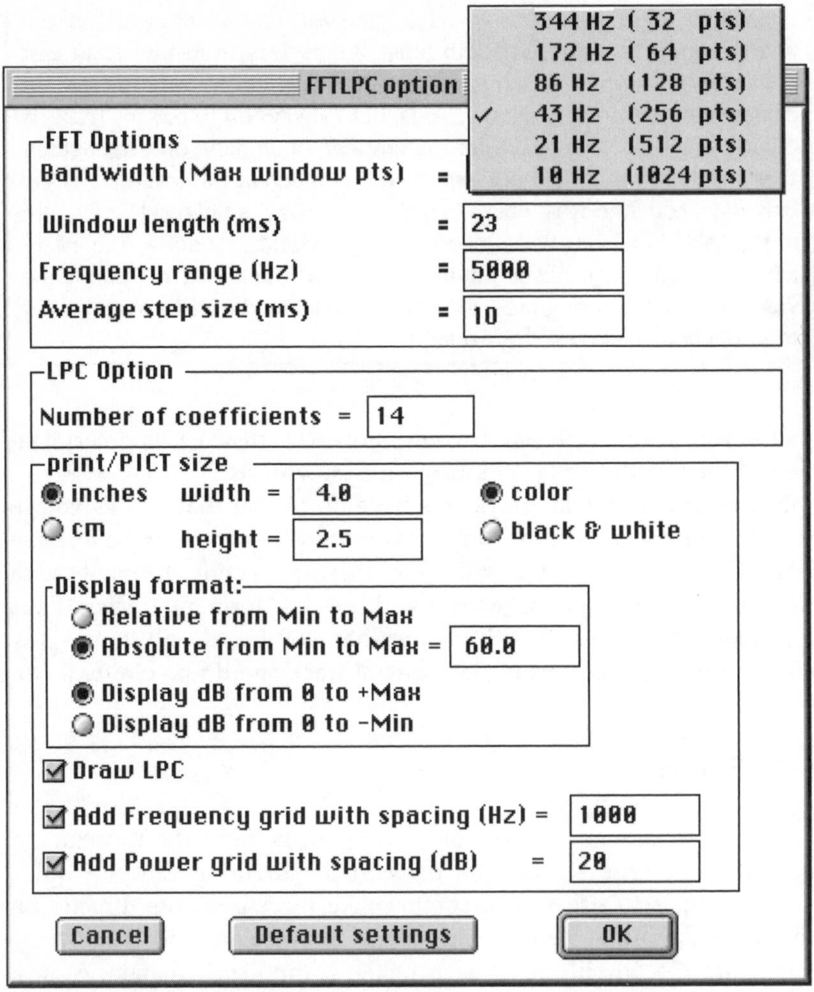

344 Hz	(32 pts)
172 Hz	(64 pts)
86 Hz	(128 pts)
✓ 43 Hz	(256 pts)
21 Hz	(512 pts)
10 Hz	(1024 pts)

FFTLPC option

FFT Options

Bandwidth (Max window pts)   =

Window length (ms)   =   23

Frequency range (Hz)   =   5000

Average step size (ms)   =   10

LPC Option

Number of coefficients = 14

print/PICT size

⦿ inches   width =   4.0   ⦿ color

◯ cm   height =   2.5   ◯ black & white

Display format:
◯ Relative from Min to Max
⦿ Absolute from Min to Max =   60.0

⦿ Display dB from 0 to +Max
◯ Display dB from 0 to -Min

☑ Draw LPC

☑ Add Frequency grid with spacing (Hz) =   1000

☑ Add Power grid with spacing (dB)   =   20

[Cancel]   [Default settings]   [OK]

Figure 5.10   Options to be considered when making spectra.

32 points in the sampled wave when calculating the frequencies that are present. This sound was sampled at 11,000 Hz, not 22,000 Hz as in the spectrograms considered earlier (11,000/32 = 344). This makes it fairly precise in the time domain, at the expense of not separating out the individual harmonics. They are lumped together, just as they were in the wideband spectrograms in figure 5.2. The narrowband spectrum on the right of figure 5.11, using a bandwidth of 21 Hz and

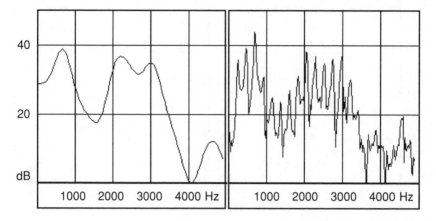

Figure 5.11 A spectrum with a bandwidth of 344 Hz on the left, and with a bandwidth of 21 Hz on the right, made in the middle of the vowel in *head* as spoken by a female speaker.

a window with 512 points, separates out the component harmonics of the sound.

Which of the two spectra in figure 5.11 provides the better way of locating the formants? There is no clear-cut answer to this question, and, as we will see, neither of them is the preferable way of making consistent measures of formant frequencies. The wideband spectrum on the left allows you to find the formant peaks at about 650, 2,250 and 3,000 Hz in this particular vowel. In other vowels the first formant may be close to the fundamental frequency, so that there is no clear peak corresponding to the first formant, or two formants may be too close together. The narrowband spectrum on the right shows the harmonics, which is sometimes useful, but in order to determine the formant peak you have to imagine a curve going smoothly around the highest harmonics. In this case such a curve should show that the formant peak is between the second and third harmonics (the two highest harmonics) but closer to the third (highest) harmonic.

When the formants are close together, as in the spectra of the vowel shown in figure 5.12, neither the wide- nor the narrowband spectrum gives a good indication of the formant frequencies. (This is the same vowel as shown in the spectrogram in figure 5.7.) The first two formants appear as a single peak below 1,000 Hz. Their frequencies cannot be determined from these spectra.

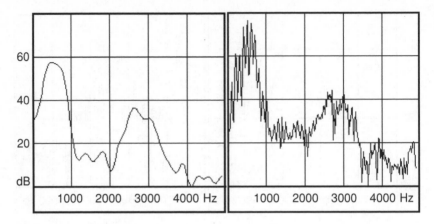

Figure 5.12 A spectrum with a bandwidth of 173 Hz on the left, and with a bandwidth of 21 Hz on the right, made in the middle of the vowel in *caught* as spoken by a male speaker.

Fortunately there is another way in which the formants can be determined. Rather than trying to locate peaks in the wide- or narrowband spectra it is possible to get the computer to calculate the formant frequencies derived from a so-called LPC spectrum. The option to use is shown near the bottom of figure 5.10, 'Draw LPC spectrum'.

The spectra we have been considering so far have all employed a form of Fourier analysis. This analysis makes no presumptions about how many (if any) formants are present. It just determines the amount of energy at each different frequency, leaving the user to decide which peaks in the spectrum correspond to formant peaks. The alternative method of determining formant frequencies, LPC (Linear Predictive Coding), works explicitly in terms of a certain number of peaks (referred to as poles) corresponding to the formants. It assumes that the wave can be described as the sum of a number of formant poles, and then determines which set of poles (formant frequencies and amplitudes) would fit this wave with the least possible error. (This is not a description of the mathematical procedure, but it is in effect what happens. If you want to know more, see the second edition of my *Elements of Acoustic Phonetics*.)

Figure 5.13 shows the same spectra as in figure 5.11 (the middle of the vowel in *head* as spoken by a female speaker), but with the LPC spectrum superimposed. Note that the LPC spectrum provides

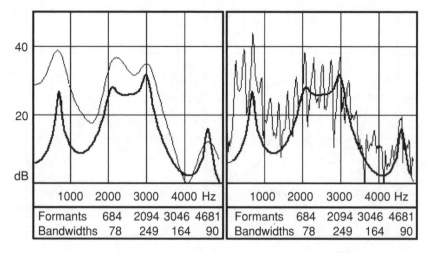

Formants	684	2094	3046	4681	Formants	684	2094 3046	4681
Bandwidths	78	249	164	90	Bandwidths	78	249 164	90

Figure 5.13 The same spectra as in figure 5.11 but with LPC spectra (heavy line) superimposed, and the LPC-calculated formants listed below.

a slightly different picture of where the formants are in comparison with the wideband spectrum on the left. The first formant pole in the LPC spectrum is slightly higher, a little bit closer to the highest harmonic in the narrowband spectrum on the right, and the second formant pole slightly lower, again closer to the highest harmonic in the narrowband spectrum. Which analysis is right, the formant peaks that can be seen and measured in the wideband spectrum or those calculated in the LPC spectrum?

It is difficult to say which is right. Each analysis makes different assumptions about how to calculate a spectral curve, taking the energy in the fundamental frequency and the influence of spurious formants into account in different ways. If the purpose of formant analysis is to determine as much as we can about the actions of the tongue and lips, then the spectral contributions of the fundamental frequency and spurious formants should be minimized. The amount of energy in the fundamental frequency is a complex matter, depending on the nearness of F1 to the fundamental and on the glottal state. If the vocal folds are vibrating loosely, producing some breathiness, the fundamental frequency will have a greater intensity relative to the higher frequencies, and there will also be added tracheal resonances. (Breathy voice will be discussed more fully in chapter 7.) In addition, slight

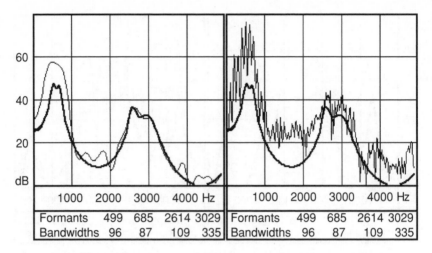

| Formants | 499 | 685 | 2614 3029 | Formants | 499 | 685 | 2614 3029 |
| Bandwidths | 96 | 87 | 109 335 | Bandwidths | 96 | 87 | 109 335 |

Figure 5.14   The same spectra as in figure 5.12 with LPC spectra (heavier line) superimposed, and the LPC-calculated formants.

nasalization will affect the spectrum by introducing resonances associated with the nasal tract. If we are concentrating on the vocal tract shape as reflected in the actions of the tongue and lips, we need to find the formant frequencies associated with these actions. But it is not clear which analysis does this better.

What is clear, however, is that it is possible to get more consistent results by allowing the computer to find the formants in the LPC spectrum than by trying to find the peaks in the spectrum yourself. The computer algorithm provides the values of the formant frequencies and bandwidths (which together form the so-called roots of the LPC equation). This is especially convenient when two formants are close together. Figure 5.14 shows the same spectra as in figure 5.12, the middle of the vowel in *caught*, with a wideband spectrum on the left and a narrowband spectrum on the right. The same LPC spectrum (heavier line) is superimposed on both FFT spectra. The first two formants are close together, but they are clearly resolved by the LPC analysis. The third and fourth formants are also distinguished.

Unfortunately, what the computer algorithm determines as the set of formants is not always what we would select through our knowledge of where to look for formants. To understand why this is so, we must examine the notions behind LPC analysis a little more. One

When I was recording sets of vowels in Defaka, a language spoken by a few hundred people on some islands in the Niger delta, the village chief gathered a group together and we sat around in a small hut. Such a formal gathering had to begin with a libation, so we sent out for a bottle of the local liquor. Some was solemnly spilled on the floor with a prayer and then the bottle was passed around. My colleague, Kay Williamson, advised me to let the liquor touch my lips and simply pretend to swallow. It was good advice; even the outside of my lips were stung.

of the options in figure 5.10 sets the number of coefficients used in the LPC calculation. This determines how many formant poles are calculated (not all of which are displayed). Generally speaking, you need two coefficients for each formant, and two more to account for higher formants. (Some people have suggested that you need a further two coefficients to account for a peak associated with the glottal source.) If the sampling rate is 11,200 Hz, the calculation range will extend to half that (5,600 Hz). Accordingly, we can expect to find 5 or 6 formants, and the default for the LPC calculation (without considering a peak due to the glottal source) is set to 14 coefficients ($6 \times 2 + 2$). To see how this works we will consider the analysis of the third vowel in figure 5.9 (the Assamese vowel with a spurious formant).

Figure 5.15 shows the result of using a different number of coefficients in the analysis of this particular ɛ vowel in Assamese. The top left panel is the default analysis, with both the narrowband FFT spectrum and the LPC spectrum being shown. You can see a local peak in the FFT spectrum (marked by an arrow) associated with what we are regarding as a spurious formant. The question at issue is whether the LPC analysis will fit a formant to this peak.

In the other panels, so as to reduce the complexity, only the LPC spectrum is shown. When there are 10 coefficients, the calculation looks for 5 formants. The top right panel of figure 5.15 shows the LPC spectrum that is generated. There are four formants in the frequency range displayed, and presumably an additional one in the higher frequencies. This is a plausible-looking spectrum for this vowel, and the formants listed below the spectrum have reasonable values for an ɛ vowel. If there are 12 coefficients, as in the lower left panel, the calculation assumes there are six formants below 5,600, and a small bend appears in the displayed spectrum. The frequency and bandwidth of the pole corresponding to this bend are reported below the spectrum,

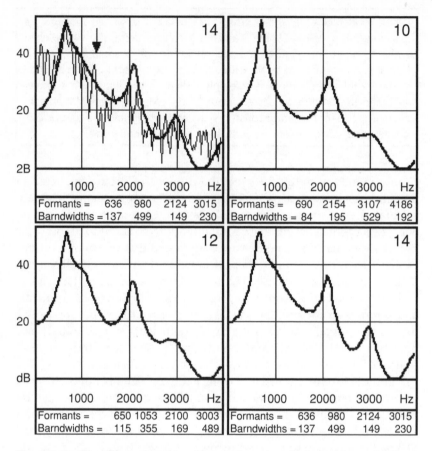

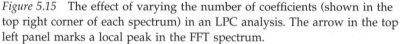

Figure 5.15 The effect of varying the number of coefficients (shown in the top right corner of each spectrum) in an LPC analysis. The arrow in the top left panel marks a local peak in the FFT spectrum.

making it appear that the second formant has a frequency of 1,053 Hz, a value that is clearly impossible for a vowel that sounds like ε. The spectrum using 14 coefficients is shown again at the bottom right, without the narrowband FFT spectrum superimposed. The slight bend in the curve corresponding to this spurious second formant is less apparent, but the frequency is listed, again making it appear that there is a second formant very close to the first formant, which we know to be not true.

Which of these analyses should you use, or, putting it another way, which of the values given for the formants are the correct ones? Once more there are no simple answers. The analysis with 10 coefficients looks good in that it shows just the four formants (with an additional higher formant outside the displayed range). But, by restricting the analysis to a small number of formants, the first peak is forced to be a pole encompassing all the energy in that region, above and below the true first formant. The analyses using 12 and 14 coefficients report distinctly lower first formant values. It is usually best to use the default number of coefficients and then, by considering the nature of the vowel and the appearance of the superimposed FFT narrowband spectrum, decide which formant frequencies to take to be representative of that vowel. Looking at the top left analysis of the vowel in figure 5.15, I would take the values of the first three formants to be 636, 2,124 and 3,015 Hz, as given by the analysis with 14 coefficients. The frequency reported at 980 Hz can be considered to be just an indicator of something about that speaker's voice quality. In further support of this conclusion we can note that the bandwidth of this extra formant is comparatively large, 499 Hz, well over double that of the other reported poles. Formant bandwidth is inversely proportional to formant intensity. Anything with a bandwidth over 400 Hz is usually insignificant.

Rewording the general statement given earlier, we can say that as a rule of thumb for a male speaker it is best to use two coefficients for each thousand or part of a thousand Hz in the calculation, and two more to account for higher formants. For a female speaker the formants will be somewhat higher, so you may need two coefficients for each 1,200 Hz in the calculation. Remember that, irrespective of the frequency range displayed, the analysis calculation will extend up to half the sample rate. So for a sampling rate of 11,200 Hz use 14 coefficients for a male speaker and 12 for a female speaker. For a sampling rate of 22,400 Hz use 20–24 coefficients. When analyzing children's speech you will need fewer coefficients as their formants are further apart, and there will be fewer of them within a given frequency range. Whenever you make an analysis, if you use a slightly larger number of coefficients than necessary, you will get some spurious formants, but you will be able to disregard them, using your human intelligence, which the computer does not have.

We should also note that in some analysis systems, the choice of the number of coefficients in the FFT/LPC options has consequences that go beyond the type of spectrum that is displayed. It also affects the Display formants choice in the Spectrogram options in figure 5.1.

Formant tracks of the Assamese vowels were shown in figure 5.9. We can now see why there were false formant tracks in this figure. The tracks were produced by making an LPC analysis every 10 ms, using the default number of coefficients. As a result some spurious formants were generated. One of the ways in which formant tracking is useful is that it indicates where FFT/LPC analyses may have problems.

The other possibilities in the FFT/LPC options shown in figure 5.10 will be considered later, when we discuss consonants and phonation types. With the exception of the window length (which should be left at its default when analyzing vowels), the additional options are mainly concerned with the appearance of the display, and do not affect the analysis.

5.3   Vowel Charts

We started this chapter by assuming we wanted to give a valid scientific description of the vowels of a language. Let's take as an example the relatively simple case of the vowels of Banawa, an Arawakan language spoken in the Amazonian rain forest. I worked on this language with a colleague, Dan Everett, who had been studying its phonology. As outlined in chapter 1, our first step was to come up with a good set of words illustrating these vowels. There are only four contrasting vowels in Banawa, so even when recording words in both stressed and unstressed syllables we did not need a long list. The words we used are shown in table 5.1. We were able to find minimally contrasting

---

The Banawa became known to people outside the Amazonian rain forest only in the 1960s. They are a very small group – about 80 people – who had little contact with others. Now that some missionaries are living with them there is an airstrip. We flew two Banawa men out to the SIL Center in Porto Velho, so that they could teach us their language. When they were not working with us they spent most of their time watching soccer on the television. The missionaries had taught them Brazil's national pastime, and they were keen fans, no doubt picking up Portuguese while they watched the game. Soon they will be using Portuguese in their discussions of soccer and all the other aspects of the world they are coming into contact with. Their children will learn to read in Portuguese; and in a generation or so Banawa will disappear.

Table 5.1   Words illustrating the vowels of Banawa in stressed syllables (the first syllable of each word) after **t** and **b**, and in unstressed syllables (the second syllable) after **f** and **b**.

Stressed		Unstressed	
tifa	drink water	**tafi**	eating
tefe	food (m.)	**tafe**	food (f.)
tafa	to eat	**tafa**	to eat
tufa	to block in	**tafu**	to eat
bita	mosquito	**ibi**	each other
befa	other	**ibe**	a strip
bata	to pick	**iba**	to put/place
bufa	put on water	**ibufa**	to dump into water

sets of words for vowels after **t** in stressed syllables and after **f** in unstressed syllables, but we were slightly less successful in finding a minimally contrasting set of words illustrating vowels after **b**. We recorded five speakers saying each of the words in table 5.1 twice. Using the techniques described above, we measured the first three formants of the most steady-state portions of each of the vowels (a total of 5 speakers with 2 tokens of 16 words = 160 vowels, 80 of them in stressed syllables).

Now let's think how you might go about using the formant frequency data. The same principles will apply to any sets of formant frequencies that you might have. The first thing you should do is to check the reliability of the measurements. When dealing with your own data you might do this by measuring everything twice. There is a problem, however, in that the error might be in deciding where a formant is located, and you might make the same mistake again when you look at the spectrogram. Ideally two different people should inspect the spectrograms and make the measurements without consulting one another.

An alternative way of checking data, and one that you can use not only with your own work but also with other people's, is to look at words that have been recorded twice. In the Banawa data you could take advantage of the fact that each word was repeated, and plot the measurements of the first utterance against those of the second. Figure 5.16 shows the results of doing this.

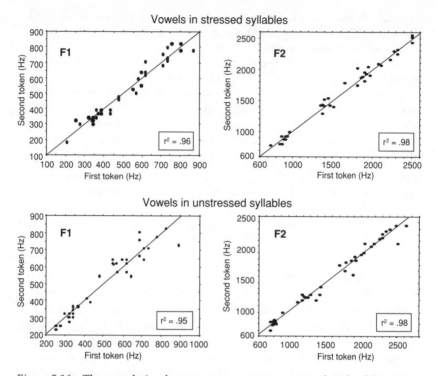

Figure 5.16   The correlation between two measurements of each of F1 and F2, one measurement in the first token of each of the words, and the other in the second token of the same word.

As you can see from the graphs in figure 5.16, the formants in the first token of each stressed vowel in a given word are much the same as those of the second token of the same word said by the same speaker. The speakers were consistent – and so were the measurements. The higher values of F1 have some differences, but those for F2 are very similar in the two repetitions of the same word. For the unstressed vowels, the F1 differences are distinctly greater, indicating either that errors have been made or that unstressed vowels are more varied in vowel height. The F2 differences for unstressed vowels are very much the same as in the case of the stressed vowels. When I was checking this data I looked at all the cases where there was more than a 50 Hz difference in any pair of vowels. I found nothing that could be rejected as being a faulty measurement, and therefore accepted the data as showing just within speaker variability.

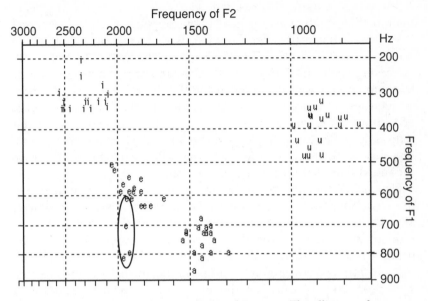

Figure 5.17   The vowels of five speakers of Banawa. The ellipse encloses four vowels of one speaker who has an aberrant /e/ vowel.

The fact that the data has been measured correctly does not show that there are no problems with the speakers. When looking at the formants of a group of people you should check whether any one speaker is different in any way from the others. Figure 5.17 is a plot of the first two formant frequencies of the stressed vowels as produced by all five speakers. The ellipse in this figure encloses the four stressed **e** vowels of speaker 4. The first formant values of his **e** vowel are, on the average, distinct from those of the other speakers. (A statistical analysis showed that they were significantly different.) Apparently this speaker pronounces this vowel in an unusual way, with a higher F1 (a more open vowel) than that of other speakers. Because his other vowels are similar to those of the rest of the speakers, the difference in this vowel cannot be ascribed to some anatomical factor such as a very small vocal tract size, which would make all the formants have a higher frequency. If you find a speaker who pronounces a word in a significantly different way, you should leave this part of the data out when providing diagrams of the vowel qualities of the language, noting, however, that there are speakers who deviate from the general pattern.

The scales in figure 5.17 are arranged so as to show the vowels in the most informative way from a phonetic point of view. Formant 1 is on the ordinate (the vertical axis), with increasing values going downwards, and formant 2 on the abscissa (the horizontal axis), with increasing values from right to left. This kind of plot arranges vowels in a similar way to the vowels in the IPA vowel chart. The formant frequencies are spaced in accordance with the Bark scale, a measure of auditory similarity, so that the distance between any two vowels reflects how far apart they sound. Because most of the energy in a vowel is usually in the first formant, the scale for this formant is more expanded than that for the second formant.

Figure 5.17 contains too many points to give the best summary of the vowel qualities in Banawa. It also does not distinguish vowels after t from those after b. The two need to be separated and some form of averaging is needed. You can make appropriate plots by using a program, such as the UCLA Plot Formants program, available at http://www.linguistics.ucla.edu/faciliti/sales/software.htm. This program will calculate the mean and standard deviation of the first two formants for each of the vowels. It will also draw an ellipse around a group of vowels with radii of two standard deviations. Given the normal statistical assumptions, this predicts that 95% of the population from which this sample of speakers is drawn will, when producing vowels like these, have formant values within this ellipse. I used the program to draw one set of ellipses around each vowel after t and another set after b, as shown in figure 5.18. Because we know the standard deviations we can say that about 95% of adult male speakers of Banawa will produce vowels that have formant frequencies that lie within the ellipses shown in figure 5.18. There are only about 30 adult male speakers of Banawa, so each of these ellipses probably holds for all save one or two of them; and we have already found one speaker who differs for one of these vowels.

Figure 5.18 provides a good description of the vowel qualities in Banawa stressed vowels. It shows that (as in most languages) vowels after b generally have lower F2 values. It also shows that in this language u is not as high as i, and might well have been interpreted as o. (In fact, one group of linguists working on Banawa chose u and another chose o.) You can use a formant chart like that in figure 5.18 to help you decide which IPA symbol to choose for whatever language you are working on.

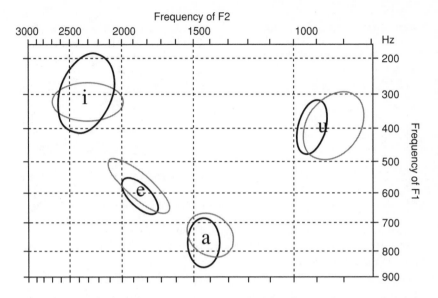

Figure 5.18   Formant plots of Banawa vowels. The ellipses drawn with solid lines show areas containing all points within two standard deviations of the mean for vowels in stressed syllables after **t**. The lighter ellipses show the same range for vowels in stressed syllables after **b**. The vowel symbols are placed at the grand mean for each vowel, irrespective of context.

A plot of F1 vs. F2 provides a good description of the vowels of Banawa and many other languages. But this kind of plot is not adequate for languages that have vowels distinguished by lip-rounding. In these cases we must take F3 into account. The acoustic dimensions repres-ented by F1, F2, and F3 do not correspond directly to the auditory/articulatory dimensions vowel height, vowel backness, and lip round-ing. In a two-dimensional plot F1 largely represent vowel height, but F2 characterizes both backness and lip-rounding. This creates a problem for phoneticians describing the vowels of languages such as French, German, Swedish, and Danish, which have front rounded vowels. The best way to show these vowels is to plot F1 vs. F3 as well as the F1 vs. F2.

Figure 5.19 shows both an F1 vs. F2 plot and an F1 vs. F3 plot of the Swedish long vowels. The data are the averages of 24 male students, as published by the Swedish phonetician Gunnar Fant. You can see that F3 helps distinguish the high front vowels **i** and **y** (arrow 1 in

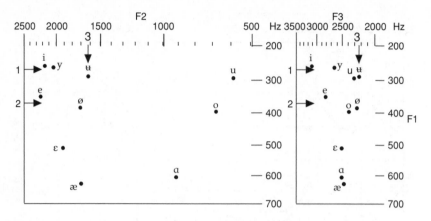

Figure 5.19   Formant plots of the Swedish long vowels (data from Fant 1973). F1 vs. F2 on the left and F1 vs. F3 on the right. The numbered arrows are referenced in the text.

figure 5.19), which have very similar F1 and F2 values. The mid high front vowels **e** and **ø** (arrow 2) are distinguished by their F2 frequencies, but they are also further distinguished by F3. The high vowel **ʉ** (arrow 3) is characterized by the lowest F3 of all these vowels. This vowel occupies a similar position on the F1 vs. F2 plot as a retracted front vowel such as English ɪ. If we were simply plotting F1 vs. F2 we would not be able to tell how it differed from English ɪ. Given that it has a very low F3 we know that it sounds very different.

Finally in connection with plotting vowels, we must consider how to represent diphthongs on a formant chart. At the beginning of this chapter I said that diphthongs should be measured near the beginning and end of the vowel, at points that are not affected by consonant transitions. This is sometimes not so easy to do. Consider the three German diphthongs in the first syllables of the words **vaɪtən**, *weiten*, 'widen'; **bɔɪtə**, *Beute*, 'booty'; **baʊtən**, *bauten*, 'built'. These syllables are shown in figure 5.20. Where are the appropriate points to measure? As we will see, it is not easy to be sure. My suggestions are shown by the lines marked (1)–(6).

The first syllable in **vaɪtən**, *weiten*, 'widen' has an initial consonant, **v**, that typically lowers all formants (although F3 is not much affected in this case). I have chosen a starting measurement point for the diphthong where the influence of the initial **v** is small, and where

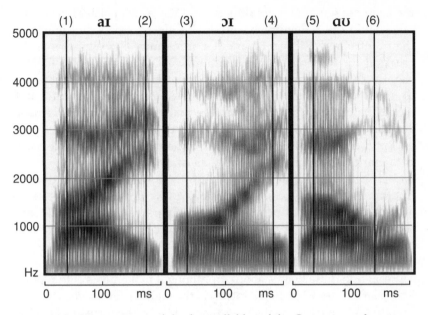

Figure 5.20   Spectrograms of the first syllables of the German words **vaɪtən**, *weiten*, 'widen'; **bɔɪtə**, *Beute*, 'booty'; **baʊtən**, *bauten*, 'built'. The numbered lines mark measurement points discussed in the text.

F2 becomes steadier and F1 approaches its maximum. Line (2) shows where I thought the diphthong ends, though it is arguable that I should have put it a little earlier, where F2 is slightly higher. This is not a straightforward decision as it involves complex articulatory acoustic relations. As the tongue moves up and forward for a high front vowel there comes a point where the resonance of the front cavity (the indicator of how front a vowel is) is associated with F3 rather than F2. But a vowel chart uses only F2 to show the front–back dimension, so perhaps we should use the F2 maximum as our final measurement point, although this is not the endpoint of the vowel. As with all measurement problems, make your decision, state your procedures and be consistent.

The second vowel, ɔɪ, as in **bɔɪtə**, *Beute*, 'booty', has a fairly steady-state portion at the beginning, and an end that is similar to the first of these three diphthongs but with F1 not going quite so low. I have shown the measurement points by lines (3) and (4). The third vowel, aʊ, as in **baʊtən**, *bauten*, 'built', presents further problems. Marking the beginning line (5) is not difficult, but it is much harder to say what one should call the endpoint of this diphthong. I have put line (6) at the point where F1 and F2 are at a minimum, choosing this as my criterion for the end of the diphthong. But after this point F1 rises slightly and F2 considerably. These increases take place over a period of time that is greater than the usual consonant transition interval. It would be quite reasonable to decide that these formant movements are part of the vowel and should be noted.

Diphthongs can be represented on formant charts. The simplest way is to mark the starting point and then draw an arrow pointing to the end. This is the technique that I and others have used in textbooks. But this leaves out a lot of information. As we noted above, the vowel ɔɪ in the second word begins with a comparatively steady state, and the third vowel, aʊ, is a complex diphthong that involves more than the movement from one place to another. Even the first vowel, aɪ, does not move at an even rate from beginning to end. One way of representing these details about diphthongal movements is to plot the values of F1 and F2 at 10 ms intervals throughout the vowel. (We saw in figure 5.10 how an analysis system can show the formants at 10 ms intervals on a spectrogram.) Instead of (or in addition to) the beginning and end points, the formant tracks for the German diphthongs can be entered into a formant plotting program. Figure 5.21 shows the results of representing these vowels both by single arrows and by formant tracks. As we noted in the spectrogram, the diphthong aʊ has an upward movement of F2 at the end, shown in the chart by the three points to the left of the arrowhead for this vowel. We can also see how the vowel, aɪ, does not move at an even rate, and the relatively small changes in F1 that occur at the beginning of ɔɪ.

For the purposes of this discussion we have been considering only a single example spoken by one speaker of each of the three German diphthongs. The results shown in figure 5.21 are therefore severely limited. We don't know if this speaker is like others, or whether these words have any peculiarities in their pronunciation. We do not even know if the measurement points that we chose for each vowel can be found in other vowels. Without further information about other speakers and other vowel contexts we cannot make any decisions about what measurements most suitably characterize German diphthongs. The best way of investigating the vowels of a language is to go through a lot of data once quickly before settling on the measurement procedures that you will use. Only after you have looked at a whole

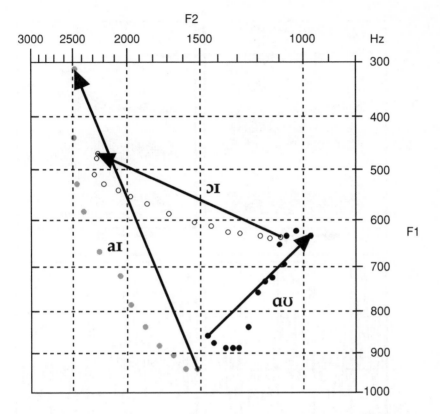

Figure 5.21   A formant chart showing the German diphthongs in the first syllables of the German words **vaɪtən**, *weiten*, 'widen'; **bɔɪtə**, *Beute*, 'booty'; **baʊtən**, *bauten*, 'built', as spoken by one speaker.

range of vowels can you decide on a measurement procedure that will fit all of the data to be analyzed.

5.4   Nasalized Vowels

In an introductory book such as this, there is little that can be said about the acoustic analysis of nasalized vowels. These vowels are characterized partly by what is there, but also by what isn't. The most obvious fact about nasalized vowels is that the first formant tends to disappear. The upper part of figure 5.22 shows spectrograms of the

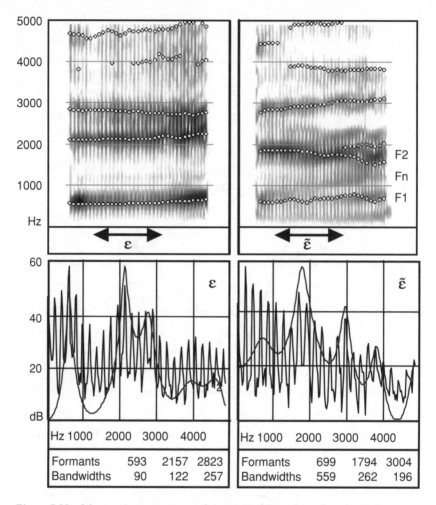

Figure 5.22 Mean spectrograms and spectra of French oral and nasal vowels cut out from the words lɛ, *laid*, 'ugly' and lɛ̃, *lin*, 'flax', averaged over the intervals shown by the arrows below the spectrogram.

vowels in the French words lɛ, *laid*, 'ugly' and lɛ̃, *lin*, 'flax'. The first formant in the vowel on the right is noticeably fainter – without the superimposed formant tracks you might have had difficulty finding it.

There are other differences between the spectrograms of the oral and nasal vowels in figure 5.22. In the area between F1 and F2 there is

some extra energy that I have labeled Fn, which is particularly noticeable towards the end of the nasalized vowel. In addition, the second
formant is considerably lower in the nasalized vowel.

The lower part of figure 5.22 shows the FFT and LPC spectra. The
peaks in the spectra found by the LPC analysis are not, strictly speaking, formant peaks, because the LPC algorithm is not applicable to
nasalized vowels. Nevertheless, they can be regarded as good measures
of the peaks of prominence in the spectrum. They are useful indicators
of what can be heard. The LPC analysis also gives the bandwidths of
what it considers to be the formants. As you can see, the first two
formants of the nasalized vowel have a much greater bandwidth –
they are less sharply defined and lower in amplitude than the corresponding formants of the oral vowel. An increased bandwidth is often
an indication of nasalization.

Finally, the analysis of these oral and nasal vowels demonstrates
another of the options available in a good speech analysis system. You
can select a section of a vowel and find the average formant frequencies. The spectra in the lower part of figure 5.22 are each the mean of
7 spectra, one every 10 ms throughout the intervals marked by the
arrows below the spectrogram. When there is a steady state in the
middle of a vowel this is a good way of ensuring that the spectral
analysis reflects the true values of the formants.

5.5   Further Reading

Stevens, K. N. (2000). *Acoustic phonetics*. Cambridge, Mass.: MIT Press.
Chapter 6, Vowels, is a comprehensive, technical account of the acoustics of
    vowels and other sounds that are produced with a relatively open vocal tract.

6

Acoustic Analysis of Consonants

The acoustic characteristics of consonants are very diverse. Some consonants, such as the semivowels **w** and **j**, are very much like vowels. They have readily distinguishable formants, differing from those of vowels primarily in that they have rapid movements and there may be no steady states. Other consonants, such as nasals and laterals, have formants that usually have a lower intensity than vowels. Fricatives have noise components that have to be investigated in a different way, as do stop bursts. Consonants also have varying places of articulation, which require yet other analytical techniques. Almost the only thing that nearly all these sounds have in common is that their durations can be measured in much the same way.

6.1 Waveforms, spectrograms, and duration measurements

Earlier I suggested that the best way to measure most aspects of duration was in terms of points on the waveform, also noting that spectrograms can provide useful supporting data in some cases. This is an appropriate moment to see how this works. Let's suppose that you want to measure the duration of each of the segments in a phrase such as *We saw birds*. (This presumes that there are such things as separable segments, a notion that, as we will see, is difficult to maintain at times.) The waveform and spectrogram of *We saw birds* are shown in figure 6.1. The waveform is illustrated again in figures 6.2–6.4 on an expanded scale.

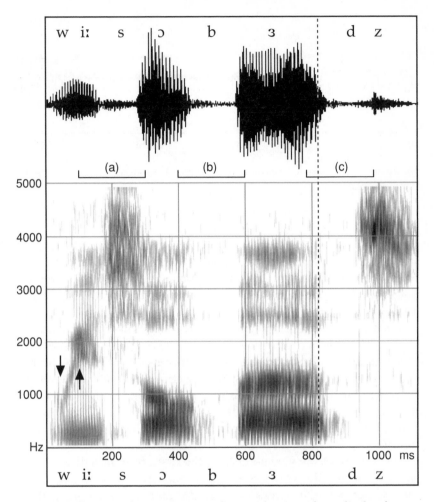

Figure 6.1   The use of a spectrogram along with a waveform display for measuring durations. The segments marked (a), (b) and (c) in the waveform mark sections that are shown enlarged in figures 6.2–6.4. The arrows and the dashed line on the spectrogram are discussed in the text.

The initial semivowel, **w**, is just a glide leading into the vowel. There is no definitive way of measuring its duration in this parti-cular example, because you cannot say where it stops. You could, arbitrarily, decide that the **w** ends at the first arrow on the spectrogram, where the second formant starts rising. Or you could decide that this

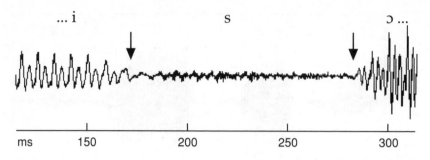

Figure 6.2   An expanded portion of the waveform marked (a) in the upper panel of figure 6.1.

movement is part of the **w**, and consider the second arrow on the spectrogram to be the end of the **w**, where the **i** formants are more or less in a steady state. Or you could decide the best measurement point is half-way between these two. There is no answer to this problem. There is no separate **w**.

It is much easier to say where the vowel **i** ends and the consonant **s** begins. The spectrogram shows that it is shortly before the 200 ms time line, but you cannot make an accurate measurement to the nearest 5 ms, because the time scale of the spectrogram is too compressed. (If you expand the time scale of the spectrogram to any great extent it blurs and becomes more difficult to read.) Figure 6.2 shows an expanded portion of the waveform marked (a) in the upper panel of figure 6.1.

The voicing of the vowel **i** ends at the first arrow in figure 6.2, and starts again for the vowel **ɔ** at the second arrow. We can take the interval between the arrows to be the duration of **s**. By looking at the scale below the waveform you can see that this is a little over 100 ms. When measured using the cursors on a computer display of the wave-form it turns out to be 114.7 ms. It is not possible to make a reliable measurement of a duration in tenths of a millisecond. As we can see in this example, the cursors (denoted by the arrows in the figure) might well have been placed slightly differently. You should always make duration measurements as accurately as you can, but report them only to the nearest 5 ms.

We next need to measure the **ɔ** in *saw*. It begins at the end of the **s**, which we have just marked in figure 6.2, and ends at the beginning of

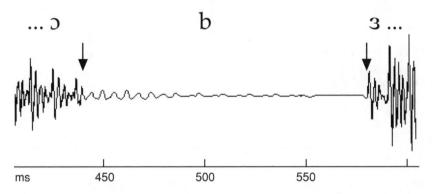

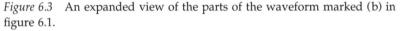

Figure 6.3   An expanded view of the parts of the waveform marked (b) in figure 6.1.

the **b** in *birds*. You can make a rough estimate of when the **b** begins by looking at the spectrogram in figure 6.1. It must be around the 450 ms mark. But it is much easier to see where the **b** begins in figure 6.3, which shows the portion marked (b) in figure 6.1. The first arrow in figure 6.3 shows where the sound wave changes shape because of the labial closure. During the vowel there is a more elaborate wave shape with a number of minor peaks within each glottal pulse. When the lips close the sound is produced within a closed vocal tract, and the waveform is smaller, with a less varied shape.

Between the arrows in figure 6.3 you can see the sound associated with the closure for the **b**. These very low-intensity vocal fold vibrations become much greater at the time of the second arrow, which is when the lips open and the **ɜ** vowel in *birds* begins. The end of that vowel can be seen in figure 6.4, which also shows the duration of the consonant **d** at the end of *birds*. The first arrow in this part of the figure marks where the consonant **d** might be said to begin, judging by both the waveform and the spectrogram. A dashed line on the spectrogram in figure 6.1 marks this same point. The first formant is still visible in the spectrogram after the dashed line, but the loss of energy in the second and higher formants suggests that the consonant constriction has been formed. For that reason I placed the first arrow in figure 6.4 at the break, leaving a fairly large glottal vibration visible at the beginning of the consonant closure.

Finally, can we say anything about the duration of the **z** (phonetically **s**) at the end of *birds*? Looking at the spectrogram as well as the

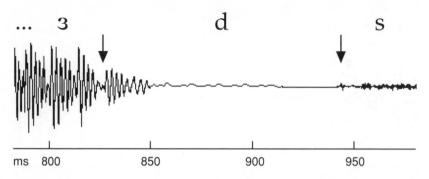

Figure 6.4   An expanded view of the parts of the waveform marked (c) in figure 6.1.

waveform I took it that it began at the time indicated by the second arrow in figure 6.4. But I may well be wrong. There are inherent uncertainties in the measurement of duration, and, even if the beginning of this sound is correctly marked, it fades away so that its end cannot be delimited with precision. Because I would never try to measure the end of a final fricative of this kind, I have not attempted to show it on either the spectrogram or the waveform.

Measuring successive segments is a task that is necessary on some occasions, such as when trying to give an exhaustive account of a phrase, but a more typical use of duration measurements is for distinguishing different possibilities among stops. Many languages contrast aspirated and unaspirated voiceless stops that are distinguished by their Voice Onset Time (VOT), a feature that we discussed in chapter 4. In that discussion we also noted that it is often difficult to decide exactly when a given phenomenon – the release of a stop or the start of vocal fold vibration – occurs. The acoustic record can be read in different ways, and choices have to be made. It's worth repeating that what matters in measuring data is to devise a plan, write it down, and keep to it. When measuring VOT, does the vowel start at the first sign of an increase in amplitude in the waveform, or only when a full cycle can be seen? Similarly, when measuring vowel length, are you going to count the aspiration after a stop as part of the vowel, or will you say that the vowel begins when voicing starts? (Some studies do one, others the other; I even know of one study that suggested considering half of the aspiration as part of the consonant and half as part of the vowel.) Is the end of a voiceless fricative between vowels at the point when the frication noise ends, or when the voicing for the vowel begins, which may be after a short period of aspiration? (Again, studies vary.) There are no correct answers to questions like these. If there is any published work comparable to the study you are undertaking, consider using the same technique. In any case, make sure you measure everything in the same way.

6.2   Spectral characteristics of nasals, laterals, approximants, and trills

Nasals are usually easy to spot on spectrograms. Figure 6.5 shows spectrograms of the three English nasals in *simmer, sinner, singer.* Each of these nasal consonants has a bar near the base line, indicating energy at around 200 Hz. In the case of **m**, in the upper spectrogram, and **ŋ**, in the lower spectrogram, there is also a faint formant at a little over 2,000 Hz. For the alveolar nasal **n** in the middle spectrogram, there is some energy present in the 2,000 Hz region, but it is even fainter.

Because nasals have a lower amplitude than vowels, their formants are often not fully visible in regular spectrograms. You can overcome this problem, as I did in figure 6.6, which is a spectrogram of the nasals at the ends of the words *ram, ran, rang.* I increased the intensity range displayed in the spectrogram by 15 dB. This makes the nasals more clearly visible, but the vowels are a little too dark to make it easy to see the exact locations of their formants. Setting the intensity range for a spectrogram is one of the options available in an analysis program, as was illustrated in figure 5.3 in the previous chapter.

The low frequency formants near 200 Hz, and the formants above 2,000 Hz in figure 6.6 have been marked by solid lines. Increasing the intensity range brings up additional resonances that are not normally visible. Dashed lines have been added to the spectrograms showing that each of these nasals has a distinct formant in the 1,000 to 2,000 Hz range. This faint formant is at about 1,100 Hz for the bilabial **m**, slightly higher for the alveolar **n**, and from about 1,700 to 2,000 Hz for the velar **ŋ**. This formant corresponds to a resonance of the body of air behind the closure. The frequency increases as the closure moves back and the size of that body of air decreases. We can even see a rise in frequency during the velar nasal **ŋ**, indicating that the tongue moved further back during the pronunciation of this sound. A measurement

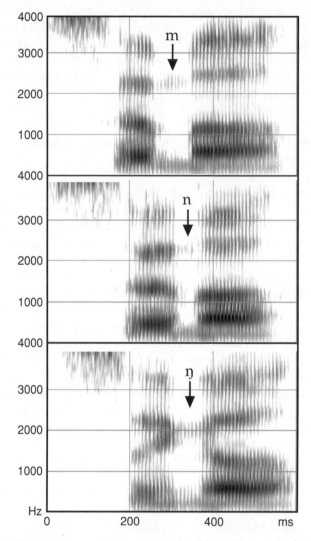

Figure 6.5 Spectrograms of *simmer, sinner, singer.*

of this formant frequency could be used to distinguish the place of articulation of the nasals, but it is usually too low in amplitude to be measured reliably. The movements of the formants in the surrounding sounds are a better guide to the place of articulation differences, as we will see in section 6.4.

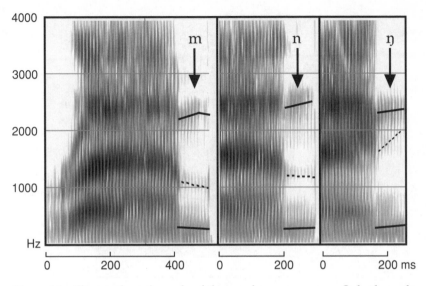

Figure 6.6   The nasals at the ends of the words *ram*, *ran*, *rang*, Only the ends of the last two words are shown.

From an acoustic point of view, laterals are like nasals in that they have formants with lower amplitudes and with distinct locations from those in the neighboring vowels, usually producing an abrupt break in the pattern. Laterals differ from nasals in that their formants (particularly the second formant) more readily show distinctions among them. Thus the difference between a palatal and an alveolar place of articulation is plainly evident (and can be measured) in the laterals in Bura, a Chadic language spoken in Nigeria (figure 6.7). The palatal lateral at the beginning of the Bura word ʎ̥álá 'cucumber' is phonologically voiceless, but, as is often the case with contrasting voiceless nasals and laterals, there is a short voiced section before the vowel begins (marked by an arrow to the left of the first dashed line). The second formant in this sound has a frequency near 2,000 Hz, distinguishing it from the alveolar lateral in the middle of the word (shown by a heavy line), which has a frequency of about 1,300 Hz.

In a similar way, differences in the frequencies of F2 can be used to quantify the degree of palatalization and velarization in English laterals. Figure 6.8 shows a comparison of the words *feel* and *leaf* in my pronunciation. Beginning students often have the naive notion that these

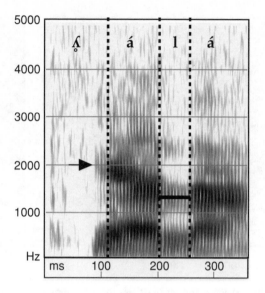

Figure 6.7   A voiceless palatal lateral and a voiced alveolar lateral (marked by dashed lines) in the Bura word ʎ̥álá 'cucumber'. The arrow and the heavy line mark the second formants of the two laterals.

words contain the same sounds in the reverse order, but as the spectrograms show, they do not. The final velarized ł in *feel* has a low F2 at around 800 Hz, whereas the so-called clear l in *leaf* has a high F2 at about 1,200 Hz.

As a further example of the analysis of laterals, consider a more difficult case, the velar lateral in Melpa, an Indo-Pacific language spoken in Papua New Guinea. Figure 6.9 shows the alveolar lateral that occurs in Melpa words such as **lola** 'to mutter' and the more unusual velar lateral in the Melpa word **paʟa** 'fence'. As the arrows above the figure show, the alveolar laterals in the left-hand word are easy to segment. The sharp break in the locations of the formants and the differences in intensity indicate where these sounds begin and end, and you could easily measure their durations. The velar lateral in the right-hand word, however, is not so clearly delineated, partly because there is some added fricative noise. In this unusual sound the tongue is narrowed and makes contact with the soft palate over a comparatively large area. Air escapes at the sides, but towards the end of this particular articulation there is complete contact forming a brief velar plosive.

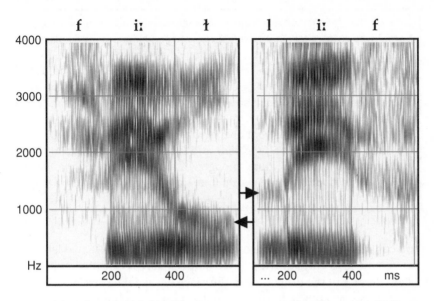

Figure 6.8   The words *feel* and *leaf* in my pronunciation. The arrows indicate the position of F2 in the laterals, comparatively high for the l in *leaf*, and lower for the velarized ɫ in *feel*.

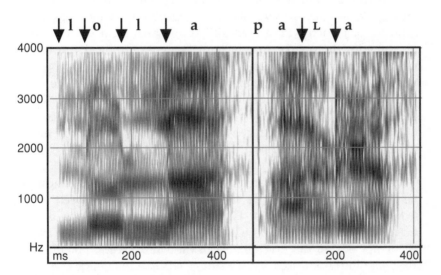

Figure 6.9   Alveolar laterals in the Melpa words **lola** 'to mutter' and a velar lateral in the Melpa word **paʟa** 'fence'.

One of the delights of lecturing in foreign universities is how much I learn. I was giving a talk in the University of Papua New Guinea, explaining (probably too pompously) what sounds could and could not occur. I said that no language has a velar lateral involving contact between the back of the tongue and the center of the soft palate and air escaping past the sides of the tongue. A hand shot up and a speaker of Melpa said, 'But my language does.' I heard him say a couple of words and instantly asked him to come to the front and let me look into his mouth. I got out my flash light (always be prepared) and looked as he said [paʟa], the word meaning 'a fence'. Sure enough, he narrowed his tongue while making contact with the soft palate in the center. It was a genuine velar lateral.

You can measure the differences in duration between these two laterals. You could also measure the brief stop closure associated with the velar lateral. But the difference in the place of articulation is not readily quantifiable in acoustic terms. The palatographic techniques discussed in chapter 2 are more useful in this respect.

Other approximants, such as **w**, **ɹ**, **j**, also have spectra with formants that can be measured, but there are no steady states. Consider that charming English sentence containing only approximants and vowels, *We owe you a yoyo*, shown in figure 6.10, which has three instances of **j**, each with a high F2 like the high front vowel **i**. You can quantify the degree to which the tongue is moved towards a high front position by measuring the frequency of F2. As you can see, F2 is highest (2,940 Hz), and therefore the tongue is in the most high front position, for the initial stressed consonant in *yoyo*. F2 is slightly lower (2,810 Hz), and the tongue slightly retracted and lower, for the beginning of *you*. It is even lower for the second consonant in *yoyo* (2,740 Hz), which has the weakest articulation of these three occurrences of **j**.

Similar measurements can be used to quantify the closeness of the articulation in **w**, but this time what should be measured is the decrease in the frequency of F2, an indicator of the degree of lip-rounding. Figure 6.11 shows a spectrogram of *We weeded the wheat*, with emphasis on the first syllable of the word *weeded*. For the first consonant in this stressed word F2 descends to a low value (520 Hz). For the first consonant in *wheat* it does not go below 750 Hz, and we can conclude that the lips were less rounded.

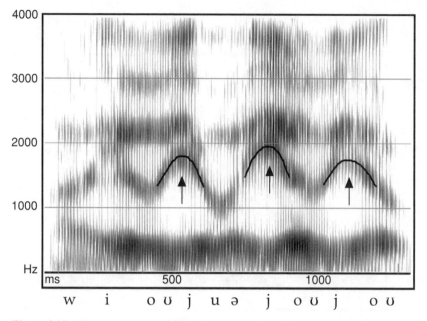

Figure 6.10   A spectrogram of *We owe you a yoyo*. A broad transcription has been used for the vowel qualities. A line has been drawn through parts of the second formant. The arrows indicate the highest points of F2, when the tongue is most raised towards the hard palate.

Another approximant with clearly visible formants is ɹ, as in English *red*, which is usually marked by a decrease in the frequency of F3. Variations in the frequency of F3 indicate the degree of r-coloring: the lower the F3, the greater the degree of rhoticity. Figure 6.12 shows the phrase *A red berry*. At the time of the first arrow, F3 descends to 1,240 Hz for the initial ɹ in *red*, which was the stressed syllable in this

---

Sentences like *We owe you a yoyo* were well known to many of us in the early days of speech synthesis, when our synthesizers were not very good at making consonants. At one meeting I remember somebody asking us to get ready to write down what we heard when he played a recording of his latest piece of speech synthesis. Somebody said, 'Wait a minute. Let's try to write it down *before* we hear it.' Several of us wrote down *We were away a year ago*. We guessed correctly which of the well-known sentences he was trying to synthesize.

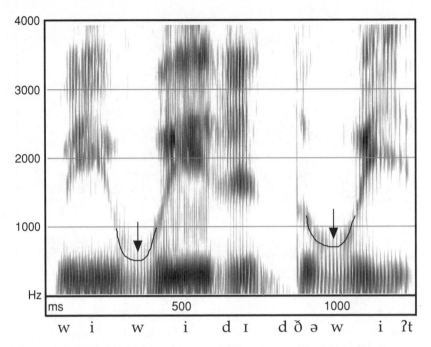

w   i   w   i   d   ɪ   d   ð   ə   w   i   ʔt

Figure 6.11   A spectrogram of *We weeded the wheat*, said with emphasis on *weeded*. A line has been drawn through parts of the second formant. The arrows indicate the lowest points of F2, when the lips were most rounded.

phrase. There is a large decrease in F3 because the tongue makes a considerable movement for this sound, the first consonant in a stressed syllable. But F3 goes down only a little, to 2,100 Hz, for the intervocalic ɹ in *berry*, marked by the second arrow. We can conclude that this intervocalic consonant has only a small tongue movement. (We should note that F3 lowering can be used in this way, as a measure of the raising and retraction of the tip of the tongue, but it can also be due to bunching the tongue and retracting the tongue root, narrowing the pharynx. The lowering of F3 in retroflex stops and laterals is illustrated later in this chapter.)

While we are considering forms of **r**, we should also note that spectrograms are useful when trying to distinguish between taps and trills. Figure 6.13 shows the distinction between the Spanish words **peɾo**, *pero*, 'but' and **pero**, *perro*, 'dog'. There is a single tap of the tongue in the first word, marked by an arrow, and a trill that might be

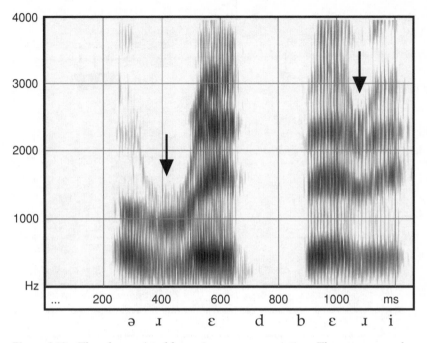

Figure 6.12   The phrase *A red berry*, in my pronunciation. The arrows mark the centers of the ɹ sounds.

considered to consist of three taps of the tongue in the second word. The spectrogram shows that there is also what might be considered as a fourth tongue movement, a vibration of the tongue that doesn't make contact with the roof of the mouth, which I have marked with a dashed arrow.

When you are describing a language that has a distinction between a short and a long trill, spectrograms can also be useful. Finnish distinguishes between a single trill in **puran** 'I undo' and a long, or geminated, trill in **purra** 'to bite', as shown in figure 6.14. In the first word there are two taps of the tongue forming the trill, and in the second there are four. You can calculate the rate of the tongue movements by measuring the length of each vibration. In the second Finnish word they averaged 44 ms each. (I made the measurements on the waveform, which, as discussed earlier in this chapter, is easier than on the spectrogram.) This indicates that the tongue tip is vibrating at a rate of 1,000/44 = 22.7 Hz, a fairly typical rate for a trill.

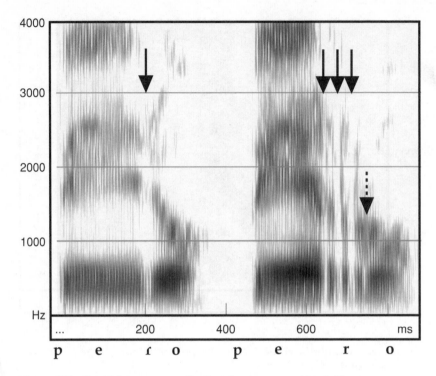

Figure 6.13 Spanish **pe.ro**, *pero*, 'but' and **pero**, *perro*, 'dog'. The arrows marking the tap ɾ and the trill r are discussed in the text.

6.3   Fricatives and Stop Bursts

Voiceless fricatives have fairly distinct acoustic characteristics. Figure 6.15 is a spectrogram of **s** in *sigh* and ʃ in *shy* as pronounced by a female Californian speaker (most of the vowel has been cut off, as we are concentrating on the consonants). We can make several remarks about the general appearance of the fricative noise in these spectrograms. The **s** has most energy above 6,000 Hz. The major concentration of energy appears to be between 8,000 and 9,000 Hz, but we cannot be sure of this as the display goes up to only 10,000 Hz, at which point there is still a great deal of energy. There might be another major concentration of energy at some higher frequency. (Higher-fidelity recording equipment and a sampling rate above 22,000 Hz would, in fact, reveal small regions of energy between 10,000 and

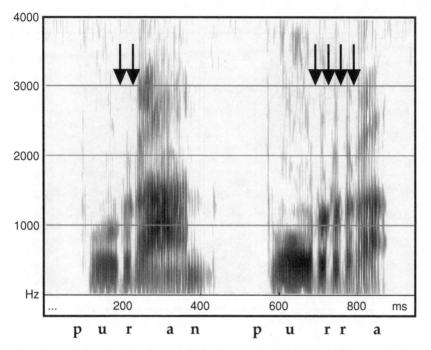

Figure 6.14   Finnish **puran** 'I undo' and **purra** 'to bite'. The arrows mark the two taps in the first word and the four taps in the second word.

14,000 Hz, but here we are considering a more typical fieldwork recording, in which the frequencies recorded do not extend so high.) The ʃ has more energy in the lower frequencies, with a considerable amount between 3,000 and 4,000 Hz, and a further band between 7,000 and 8,000 Hz. Again, there might be more energy at frequencies above 10,000 Hz, but it looks as if the energy is falling away in the higher frequencies. All these are vague remarks, and we must now consider how they can be made more precise.

The obvious way to start quantifying the characteristics of fricatives is by making a spectrum, just as we did when we wanted to measure the formants of vowels. Fricatives have a quasi-random distribution of energy. An analysis made at one instant would find energy at different frequencies from an analysis at a later moment. If we want to characterize the fricative appropriately we should consider the average spectrum over a substantial portion of the duration. The

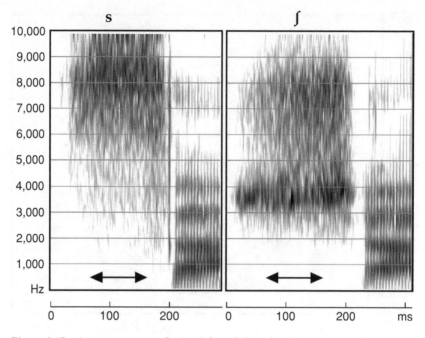

Figure 6.15   A spectrogram of **s** in *sigh* and ∫ in *shy*. The arrows indicate parts of the fricatives selected for further analysis.

arrows in figure 6.15 delimit 100 ms intervals that can be considered typical of the major part of each fricative.

But how should we make the spectra? As we saw in the discussion of how to find the formants in vowels, there are options to be considered. Because of the semi-random nature of fricative noise, it is advisable to take an average of several FFT spectra, each using a long window. A window length of 1,024 points is appropriate, with a sample rate of 22,050. This corresponds to an interval of 46 ms. We want to have a number of these 46 ms windows. If we select 100 ms in the middle of the fricative, as indicated in figure 6.16, we can place one of the 46 ms windows at the start of the 100 ms piece of the wave which is to be analyzed. We can then move the window along by 5 ms, and make another analysis. We can repeat this process until we have 11 windows, defining 10 intervals of 5 ms, as shown in figure 6.16. If we had made another move of 5 ms, the left edge, the start of the window, would have moved over 55 ms, which would

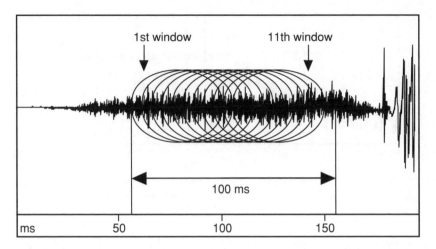

Figure 6.16   The procedure for placing 11 windows, each 46 ms long, at 5 ms intervals within a selected interval of 100 ms.

make the right edge of the window 55 + 46 = 101 ms from the start of the piece to be analyzed.

Figure 6.17 shows the result of calculating the mean FFT spectra (thin lines) for the two fricatives in figure 6.15. These very jagged shapes are difficult to characterize in a way that allows us to compare one fricative with another. Fricatives are not like vowels, which are well described by their formant frequencies. Instead, different types of fricatives have different features that are important in their auditory perception. For sibilant fricatives such as **s** and **ʃ**, the most important attributes may be the lower edge of the spectrum and the center frequencies of the peaks in the spectrum. A glance at figure 6.17 shows that these properties are not easy to measure precisely, and we must seek other techniques for producing reliable numbers to characterize fricatives.

An FFT spectrum such as that used in figure 6.17 is an analysis of a sound wave in terms of the amplitudes of a number of components. In the case of a wave sampled at 22,050 Hz, using a window of 1,024 points, which corresponds to a duration of 46 ms, the FFT will report the amplitudes of 512 components, each component being 21 Hz apart. In the fricatives we are analyzing, each of these 512 amplitudes may be very different from its neighbors, even when each is the mean of a

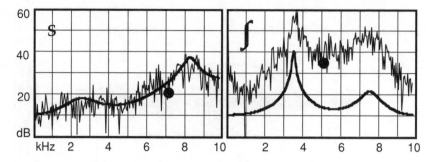

Figure 6.17   FFT spectra (thin lines) and LPC spectra (heavy lines) of **s** in *sigh* and ʃ in *shy*. The solid points show the centroids (see text).

number of adjacent windows. As a result the FFT curve has a very rough appearance.

Another way of describing fricatives is to make an LPC spectrum, which is shown using thick lines in figure 6.17. An LPC analysis arrives at a spectral curve in a very different way. It assumes that the wave can be described as the sum of a small number of poles (peaks in the curve), each peak having a certain frequency and a certain bandwidth (loosely, degree of peakedness). The LPC calculation then determines which poles (frequencies and bandwidths) would fit this wave with the least possible error.

The problem with using an LPC analysis is that before you begin the analysis you have to know how many peaks ought to be used to describe the curve. If you simply want to use the LPC analysis to get a smooth spectral curve, then you can do this by using an artificially large number of peaks, say 20. This would require setting the options so that the LPC has 40 components (a pair for each peak, one number specifying the frequency and the other the bandwidth). But if you want to specify the major peaks in the curve, as in figure 6.17, then you should set the options for 6 LPC components, giving you two peaks in the curve and a peak with a higher, off the scale, frequency. In the Macquirer/PCquirer system the options are set in the dialog box shown in figure 5.10.

Another possible way of describing one of the main aspects of a fricative spectrum is to specify the first spectral moment or centroid, the center of gravity of the shape defined by the curve and its boundaries. This is equivalent to the point on which a piece of cardboard with the shape of the curve would balance on a pin. The procedure for calculating the centroid can be illustrated by reference to the data in table 6.1, which shows the intensities at every 1,000 Hz in the smooth LPC spectrum of s in figure 6.17. In a more exact calculation of the centroid the intensity of every component in the spectrum would be used in the calculation. This table, with data at only selected frequencies, is used simply to demonstrate the procedure.

The first step is to make the intensity measurements relative to the minimum intensity, which in this case is at 1,000 Hz. The third column shows the result of subtracting this minimum, 11.5 dB, from each intensity. Next, sum the relative intensities of all the available frequencies (10, in this case), and then calculate the mean (divide the sum by 10). For the final column, multiply each frequency by the relative dB at that frequency, producing a column of weighted frequencies (Hz × dB) as shown. Sum this column and find the mean. The centroid is the result of dividing this mean (70,100) by the mean of the relative intensities (9.7).

There is actually no need to find the means. You could simply divide the sum of the product Hz × frequency (701,000) by the sum of the relative dB (97). You get the same answer, a centroid of 7,227 for the s spectrum.

Table 6.1   Selected frequencies (Hz) and their intensities in the spectrum of s in figure 6.17.

Hz	dB	Rel. dB	Hz × rel. dB
1,000	11.5	0	0
2,000	16.2	5	10,000
3,000	17.4	6	18,000
4,000	15.6	4	16,000
5,000	16.7	5	25,000
6,000	19.0	8	48,000
7,000	24.1	13	91,000
8,000	35.1	24	192,000
9,000	30.1	19	171,000
10,000	24.2	13	130,000
sum	209.9	97	701,000
mean	20.99	9.7	70,100

Centroid frequency = mean Hz × dB / mean dB = 70,100 / 9.7 = 7,227 Hz.

The centroid of the ʃ spectrum, 5,184, is also shown in figure 6.17. It is, as is usual for this pair of sounds, lower in frequency than the s centroid. This particular token has a higher mean intensity, but this is not always the case. As we saw in chapter 4, the intensity is very dependent on irrelevant factors, such as the distance between the speaker and the microphone. The centroid for ʃ is probably not a very meaningful number, as it reflects the energy in two separate peaks.

Stop bursts differ from one another in much the same way as fricatives. We can measure these differences between stops using the same techniques that we have used for analyzing fricatives. Stop bursts, however, are very much shorter so we cannot average several spectra together. Figure 6.18 shows a spectrogram of the beginning of the word *tie* (said with some emphasis so as to make the component parts discussed here more evident). In English and other languages, there are two components associated with the release of voiceless aspirated stops, the burst and the period of aspiration that follows. The burst is very like a short fricative made at the place of articulation of the stop. The aspiration is a voiceless sound with many of the features of the following vowel. When making measurements so that we can describe stop consonants we should consider just the burst, which, as in figure 6.18, may have a duration of less than 50 ms.

If we want to analyze a stop burst by making an FFT spectrum, there are certain precautions that have to be taken. As we saw in the discussion of the analysis of vowels in the previous chapter, the accuracy with which the frequency of a spectrum is calculated is related to the number of points in the sampled sound wave in the analysis window. As we have seen, if we want the accuracy that comes with having frequencies reported at 21 Hz intervals, then we need an FFT with 1,024 points (assuming a wave sampled at 22,050 Hz). The 1,024 points will have a duration of 46 ms. In other words, the calculation will be using pieces of the wave (frames) that are 46 ms long.

If the stop burst itself were about that length (as it is in figure 6.18) it might be possible to place the cursor so as to get the whole burst, and nothing of the aspiration, in the FFT window. But it would be much safer to allow for a shorter length to be analyzed. This would also be necessary when analyzing a stop with a shorter burst. There is a method that can be used to retain the accuracy of having 21 Hz intervals between frequency components without analyzing points that

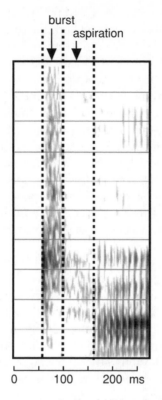

Figure 6.18   The initial consonant in *tie*, showing the difference between the burst and the aspiration.

do not form part of the burst. You can make the part of the window used in the analysis (the applied window length) less than the whole window length. You could, for example, choose to use just 23 ms (512 points out of the 1,024 in the window we have been considering). If you chose this option, the other 512 points in the 46 ms window would be set to zero (a notion known as padding the frame with zeros).

6.4   Spectrograms and Place of Articulation

Acoustic phonetic analysis is not the best way to find out about different places of articulation. You can do much better with the simple palatography techniques described in chapter 2, or even by just looking at the speaker's mouth. I've described many languages but have never found acoustic analysis useful for determining the place of articulation. It is useful for discovering what movements of the articulators might have occurred, but the place of articulation as traditionally defined is not readily apparent through acoustic analysis.

What acoustic information there is about the place of articulation of consonants is mainly available from the movements of the formants in the neighboring segments. You can see the transitions associated with different places of articulation in figure 6.19, which shows American English **b**, **d**, **g** before each of the vowels **i**, **ɛ**, **æ**, **ɑ**, **u**, as in the words *bee, bed, bad, bod, boo, D, dead, dad, dod, do, geese, get, gad, God, goo*. In each case the first 200 ms of the word is shown. As in the case of the nasals illustrated in figure 6.6, the spectrogram has been made slightly darker than usual so as to ensure that the very first parts of the transitions are visible.

The traditional notion is that F2 and F3 will rise after an initial bilabial. This is true for **i**, **ɛ**, and perhaps **æ** in figure 6.19, but it is certainly not true for **ɑ** and **u**. After an alveolar F2 is said to originate near 1,700 Hz and F3 will be level or falling from some higher frequency. This is true for most of the vowels in figure 6.19, but in the vowel **i** F2 starts at a somewhat higher value. After a velar, F2 and F3 are said to originate close together, forming what is sometimes called a 'velar pinch'. This is correct for **æ**, **ɑ**, **u** in figure 6.19, but for **i** and **ɛ** it is F3 and F4 that have a common origin. Simply measuring the so-called 'locus' frequency of each formant (the frequency of the formants at the moment where the consonant begins or ends) will not provide reliable information about the place of articulation.

The same point can be made by reference to figure 6.20, which shows the six different nasals that occur in Malayalam, a Dravidian language spoken in India. Small white lines have been placed on the second and third formants of the vowels as they move into and out of the nasals (except for the first vowel in the last word, which is different from all the others). The second formant moves downward into the bilabial nasal **m**, and both F2 and F3 move upward going out of it into the **i** vowel in accordance with the notion that bilabials have a low locus. For the dental nasal **n̪**, F2 moves up to around 1,600 Hz going into the nasal, and appears from about 1,750 Hz coming out and rising into the **i**. The transitions for the alveolar nasal **n** are very much the same, making the distinction between **n̪** and **n** hard to determine. (If I hadn't seen the speaker protruding the tongue

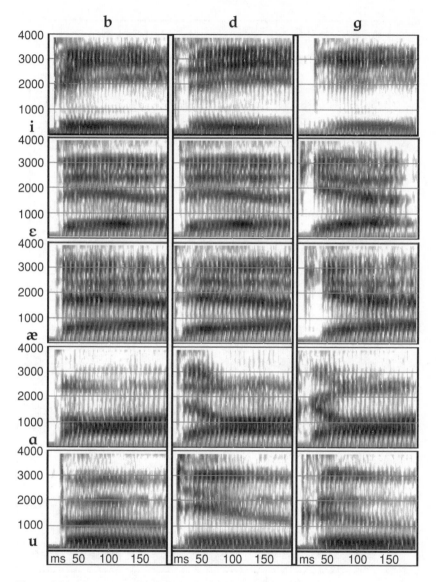

Figure 6.19   American English **b**, **d**, **g** before each of the vowels **i**, **ɛ**, **æ**, **ɑ**, **u**.

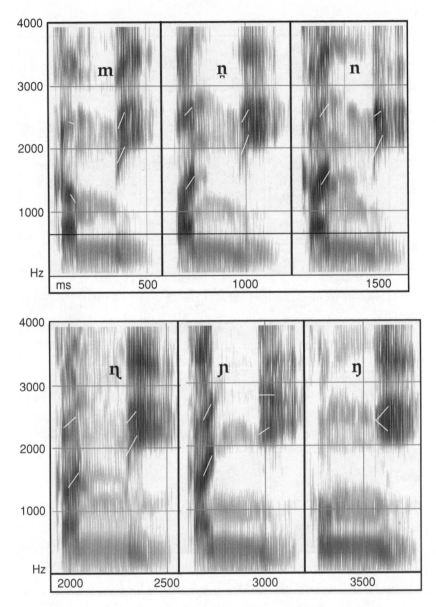

Figure 6.20   Six contrasting intervocalic nasals in Malayalam: **kʌmmi** 'shortage', **pʌn̪n̪i** 'pig', **kʌnni** 'virgin', **kʌɳɳi** 'link in chain', **kʌɲɲi** 'boiled rice and water', **kʌŋŋi** 'crushed'. The thin white lines on F2 and F3 show the formant transitions.

between the teeth when making the recording of the first word and having it more retracted for the second, I would have thought it the same sound in both words.) The transitions for the retroflex ɳ are also similar. F2 and F3 are slightly closer together and lower, but it would be difficult to make valid measurements of the differences among all the coronal consonants. The palatal nasal, ɲ, has transitions in which F2 and F3 have measurably higher frequencies than those associated with other consonants. These locus frequencies do characterize this nasal. The final nasal, ŋ, has a different vowel before it, but the same vowel after it. Coming out, the F2 and F3 are very close together, forming a velar pinch. The first vowel in this word, a high back rounded u, does not produce a velar pinch in the formants going into the consonant.

One approach to finding acoustic information that will characterize the place of articulation of a consonant is to use locus equations, a concept promoted by Harvey Sussman among others. These equations enable one to calculate an ideal locus for each consonant, provided that there is data on the formant transitions before a number of different vowels, as there is in figure 6.19. The process involves comparing the frequency of F2 at the first moment that it is visible, and at a later moment that defines the vowel quality after the release. If the vowel is a monophthong this will probably be in the middle of the vowel. For a diphthong, the defining moment will be nearer the beginning, when F1 has reached some sort of steady state. What one is aiming for is a point in time that reflects the state of the vocal tract associated with the vowel without the interference of the consonant – often an impossible notion, as the consonant gesture may be coarticulated with the whole vowel.

Figure 6.21 shows how this works out in practice for the data in figure 6.19. In each of these three graphs the frequency of F2 at its onset has been plotted against the frequency of F2 in the vowel. In each graph there are five points, one for each of the vowels. For the first consonant, **b** as in *bee, bed, bad, bod, boo*, the relationship is defined by a straight line that intersects the axis at 900 Hz, which may be regarded as an ideal, abstract, locus for this consonant. For the second consonant, **d** as in *D, dead, dad, dod, do*, there is a close relationship between the two formant measures, defined by a line that has an intercept of 1,560 Hz. This intercept forms the abstract locus characterizing this consonant. The third consonant, **g** as in *geese, get, gad, God, goo*, has a well-defined relationship for four points, which lie on a

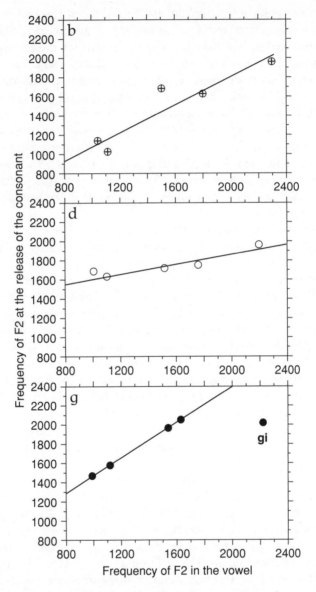

Figure 6.21　The relationship between F2 at the consonant release and in the vowel in a set of words (see text).

In the UCLA Phonetics lab we have regular lunch time sessions when we sit around trying to read a spectrogram of an unknown phrase that one of us has recorded. We often spot points that we had not previously thought about. We were, for example, looking at a spectrogram that said (unbeknownst to us) *I wear my sunglasses in bed*. We were somewhat floored by the word *sunglasses* as in this graduate student's Californian pronunciation it was pronounced as **'sʌŋlæsɪz**, as if it were *sung lasses*, with complete assimilation of the **n** to **ŋ** and with no hint of a plosive **g**. I later found that other young Californians have a similar pronunciation of this word.

straight line with an intercept of 1,280 Hz, but there is a fifth point, corresponding to the values of F2 at the beginning and in the middle of **gi** in *geese*, which is not related to the other four. This point illustrates one of the problems in calculating locus equations. The relation between vocal tract shapes and formant frequencies is very complex. Roughly speaking, during the release of a velar stop the frequency of F2 reflects the size of the cavity in the front of the mouth. However, when there is a high front vowel as in *geese*, the cavity in the front of the mouth is very small and corresponds to F3 rather than F2, which now corresponds to a higher resonance of the back cavity. Because one has to take these kinds of effects into account, and because it is hard to measure the formant frequencies at the release of a consonant, determining locus equations is often not straightforward.

6.5 Spectrograms and Articulatory Movements

So far in this chapter our main concern has been how to make measurements of acoustic analyses so that we can characterize consonants more precisely. But as has been apparent as a kind of minor theme throughout the chapter, spectrograms really come into their own when there are questions concerning articulatory movements. We saw in figure 6.6, for instance, that there is a backward movement of the tongue in the formation of this example of the velar nasal ŋ. We also noted that the velar lateral, ʟ, in figure 6.9 had a short velar stop at the end. The spectrograms concerned with the approximants j, w, ɹ in figures 6.10, 6.11 and 6.12 are primarily concerned with movements of the tongue and lips. Figure 6.13 and 6.14 reflect movements of the tip

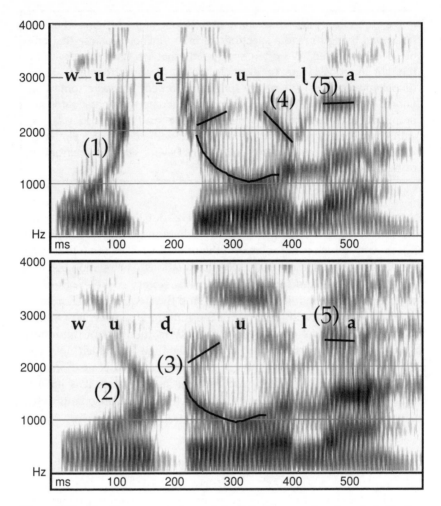

Figure 6.22   The Yanuwa words **wuḏula** 'into the grass' and **wuḍula** 'in the stomach'.

of the tongue. In figure 6.15, the spectrogram shows some aspects of English sibilants that we might not otherwise have observed. The **s** in this spectrogram has a spike at the end of the frication (almost exactly at time 200 ms) and a short gap with only aspiration before the vowel starts. This period of aspiration, with or without a sharply defined spike, is a common finding in spectrograms of fricatives. It probably occurs because there is a momentary complete closure between the tongue and the alveolar ridge, followed by a burst of noise as the tongue moves down, and another short gap before the vocal folds start vibrating. The spectrogram of ʃ in figure 6.15 does not have a spike at the end (perhaps because the aperture for this fricative is wider), but it does have a gap before the vocal folds begin vibrating. Although generally unremarked, a short period of aspiration often occurs in English fricatives.

As a further example of the use of spectrograms for gaining information about articulations, consider the spectrograms of Yanuwa, an Australasian language, in figure 6.22. There are two words, **wuḏuḷa**, 'into the grass' in the upper part of the figure with an affricated laminal post-alveolar plosive (symbolized ḏ) followed by a retroflex lateral ḷ, and **wuḍula** 'in the stomach' in the lower part, with a retroflex plosive ḍ followed by an alveolar lateral l. In the first word there is a rise in F2, marked (1) in the figure, from the **u** to the closure for the ḏ. It is this long upward sweep of F2 that shows that the tongue blade is moving up for the laminal post-alveolar stop. Now compare this articulation with the movement towards retroflex ḍ, marked (2) in the word in the lower part of the figure. During the **u** vowel there is an increase in the frequency of F2, but it is much smaller than in the movement towards ḏ. More significantly, there is also a noticeable decrease in F3. This is due to the curling up and backwards of the tip of the tongue. The formants after the release of the closure, shown by (3) and associated lines on the figure, indicate that this is an apical alveolar release, the tongue having moved during the closure. The formant transitions after the release of the stop in the upper part of the figure are much more similar to those before the stop, indicating that there is little movement during this closure.

One of my favorite memories of Australia is of the sense of humor of the speakers of aboriginal languages. A friend of mine asked a speaker if he could say, in his language, how many spears he had. None of the Australian aboriginal languages has any words for numbers other than 1 and 2, so all he could do was to list them. He said, 'Well, I have a ceremonial spear, a long throwing spear, a shorter throwing spear, a jabbing spear and a broad blade spear.' 'That makes five,' my friend said. 'If you say so,' he agreed. 'If I took one away,' my friend asked, 'how many would you have left?' 'Well,' he replied, 'it depends on which one you took away, doesn't it?'

Now consider the movements towards the retroflex lateral ɭ in the word in the upper part of the figure, marked (4). During the preceding vowel F3 falls sharply as the tongue moves up and back for the retroflex articulation. In this case it is even clearer that there is an alveolar release of this sound. As indicated by (5) in both the upper and lower parts of the figure, F3 is in a region typical of an apical alveolar articulation at this time. The sound in the upper part of the figure is a voiced retroflex flap, with the tongue moving from a tip up and back position, through a central contact in the middle of the articulation, and on to an apical alveolar release, similar to that of the sound in the lower part of the figure. One can determine all these movements by examination of the spectrograms. During the laterals l and ɭ F1 and F2 are in very similar positions, and the differences are in F3. The major distinction is in the movements into these sounds, which are well displayed in the spectrograms.

When you have only recording facilities and a computer at your disposal, you can learn a lot from acoustic analyses. You can make acoustic measurements of the durations, and some spectral features of consonants, as well as deducing what articulatory movements might have occurred. But it is worth remembering that the most useful descriptions of places of articulation are often made by palatography rather than by acoustic techniques, and that aerodynamic measures will give a more accurate account of features such as nasality and differences in air stream mechanisms than can be achieved by measuring spectrograms. You can infer a lot from spectrograms, particularly about articulatory movements that are difficult to observe in the field or in a lab that does not have access to movement-tracking facilities. But acoustic analysis is often not the best investigative technique for consonants.

6.6   Further Reading

Stevens, K. N. (2000), *Acoustic phonetics*. Cambridge, Mass.: MIT Press. Chapters 7, 8, and 9 provide technical details on the acoustics of consonants.

7

Acoustic Analysis of Phonation Types

7.1 Waveforms of Different Glottal States

How do we find out about the state of the glottis in particular speech sounds? In chapter 2 we saw that we can get some information from records of air pressure and airflow. Breathy-voiced sounds have a greater flow but less pressure than in regular voicing, and creaky-voiced sounds have the reverse. In breathy voice the vocal folds are further apart and let more air through, whereas in creaky voice they are pressed tightly together, largely blocking the airflow. We also saw in chapter 2 that electroglottography can be used to provide data on the state of the glottis. Very often, however, we cannot use aerodynamic or electro-glottographic techniques, because we no longer have access to a speaker, and all that is available is an audio recording. Acoustic analyses of ordinary audio recordings can tell us quite a lot about how the vocal folds must have been vibrating, as we will see in this chapter.

We will begin by considering breathy voice, a state of the glottis that we will define as having vocal folds that are vibrating, but loosely, so that they allow a considerable amount of breath to pass between them. This kind of voice has also been described as speaking while sighing. It is possible to have different degrees of breathiness – a very large or fairly small amount of additional air escaping in comparison with the flow of air in regular voicing ('modal' voicing, as normal phonation is called). This point is evident from figure 7.1, which shows a 150 ms section of the waveform of the word **ndæ** 'horse' in Jalapa Mazatec, an Otomanguean language spoken in Mexico. The first 50 ms

Hadza is a language spoken by a group of hunter-gatherers who have been very little influenced by other East African tribes. They have fitted their arrows with iron heads only in the last few years. While working with them we had a base camp about six miles from their settlement, in one of the more remote parts of East Africa. We often recharged our computer batteries by plugging them into a vehicle's cigarette lighter while driving back and forth. The Land-Rover broke down one day when I was driving a group of Hadza speakers back to the settlement. While one of them ran back to the base camp to get help, the others clustered around the computer. I found a game that, with their quick hand–eye coordination, they could play far better than I could within a few minutes. When my anthropologist colleague, Nick Burton-Jones, came from the base camp, he was delighted to find members of what he classified as a stone-age tribe becoming skilled computer game players.

of this section is in the upper part of the figure, the second in the middle, and the third in the lower part. The three parts are slightly overlapped so as to make it clear that this is a continuous waveform. In the first 50 ms (the upper part of the figure) the waveform is very irregular. This is because the vocal folds are apart and the airstream is being set into random variations, much like that of the wind rushing around a corner. The next section begins in this irregular way, but becomes more regular towards the end. At this time the vocal folds are approaching each other and beginning to vibrate without making a complete closure. The final section has six cycles of a repetitive waveform. Each of these cycles is produced by a glottal pulse – a sharp variation in air pressure produced when the vocal folds come together to form a complete closure. Within this display of 150 ms of the waveform we can see that in a phonologically breathy-voiced vowel the degree of breathy voicing varies from a great deal of breath and very little voice at the beginning, through a stage when the vocal folds are beginning to vibrate producing a kind of murmured voice, to a fully voiced sound in which the vocal folds are vibrating so as to produce regular glottal pulses.

The most common form of breathy voice is similar to that in the middle section of figure 7.1. Another example is shown in the upper part of figure 7.2, a section of the breathy-voiced nasal and the following vowel in the Newar word /n̤a/ 'take it'. Phonologically this word has a breathy-voiced nasal, n̤, but much of the contrast is carried by

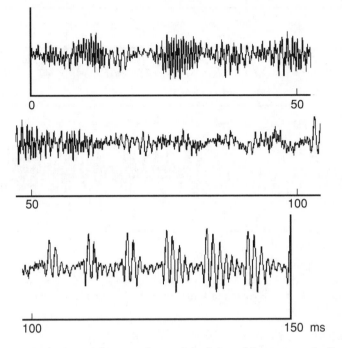

Figure 7.1   A section of the waveform of the Jalapa Mazatec word **ndæ̧**
'horse'.

the breathiness of the following vowel. There is a contrast between
this word and the regularly voiced word /**na**/ 'knead it' shown in the
lower part of the figure. The breathy-voiced waveform in the upper
part of the figure is simpler, more like a sine wave, than that in the
lower part, as you can see by comparing the sections of the waveform
marked off by the pairs of arrows. Those on the left below the waveform delimit a single period during the nasal in each case. In the lower
part of the figure, the regularly voiced nasal has two distinct peaks
within the period, plus other smaller perturbations. In the upper part
of the figure, the two peaks are less clearly distinguished, making the
breathy-voiced waveform more like that of a sine wave.

   This distinction is even more obvious when we compare the periods
in the vowels marked by pairs of arrows on the right, above the waveforms. The breathy-voiced vowel at the top is a simpler wave, with
smaller variations within the period. The regularly voiced wave below
is much more complex. We should remember, however, that this kind

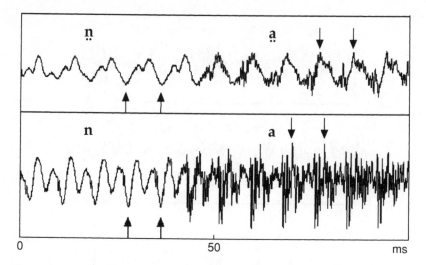

Figure 7.2   The difference between breathy-voiced and regularly voiced waveforms in the Newar word /n̪a/ 'take it' (upper part) and /na/ 'knead it' (lower part). The arrows mark off periods discussed in the text.

of distinction in the waveform – more like a sine wave for breathy voice, more complex for modal voice – is not always true. As we saw in figure 7.1, in a very breathy voice the airflow may be so turbulent that the waveform is more like random noise and there are no regular vocal fold movements.

Computer displays of the waveform also enable us to see some characteristics of creaky voice. Jalapa Mazatec has creaky vowels as well as modal and breathy vowels, so there is a three-way contrast. Figure 7.3 shows part of a creaky-voiced vowel as produced by five different speakers. The main characteristic of creaky voice that can be seen in the waveform is the irregularity of the interval between consecutive glottal pulses. We can see that the vocal fold pulses are not at exactly regular intervals of time for each of the five speakers in figure 7.3. Some speakers (e.g. speaker 1) have much more regular vocal fold vibrations than others (e.g. speaker 4), but in all cases the creaky-voiced vowel has some degree of irregularity in the intervals between glottal pulses. The technical term for this irregularity is 'jitter'.

We can quantify the degree of jitter in a vowel by using a computer program that enables us to measure the interval between adjacent glottal pulses. Using such a program we can measure the time in

Speaker

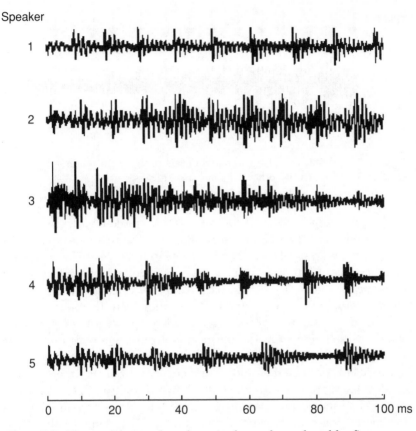

Figure 7.3   The waveforms of creaky-voiced vowels produced by five speakers of Jalapa Mazatec.

milliseconds between each of the glottal pulses for each of the speakers in figure 7.3. We can then find the average interval between pulses for each speaker. Marking the individual glottal pulses is sometimes not straightforward. It is possible to interpret the waveform of speaker 3 in different ways, particularly in the interval between 30 and 50 ms. It is always good scientific practice to try to disprove one's own hypothesis. If we try to make the measurements in the way that is most likely to disprove the hypothesis that creaky voice has irregular pulses, then the pulses for speaker 3 can be marked as shown by the solid arrows in figure 7.4. Other possible pulse onsets, which would have led to this vowel having more jitter, are marked by open arrows.

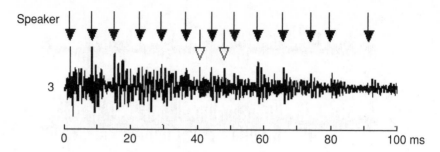

Figure 7.4   Solid arrows: the estimated onsets of the vocal pulses for speaker 3. Open arrows: other possible pulse onsets.

The next step is to see how much each speaker varies from the average. Speakers 1 and 2 vary very little from their average intervals in comparison with speakers 3, 4 and 5. These differences can be expressed in a statistical form. We can take the set of glottal pulse intervals for each speaker and calculate (or let a computer calculate) not only the mean interval but also the standard deviation from the mean.

It is, of course, also possible to calculate the degree of jitter (the standard deviation from the mean glottal pulse interval) for vowels with modal voicing. Doing this for the five Jalapa Mazatec speakers allows us to compare their modal and creaky vowels. For the speakers of Mazatec represented by the data shown in figure 7.3, creaky voice always had more jitter than modal voice. As you can see in table 7.1, the modal voices had very regular pulses. The standard deviation from the mean interval between pulses was only .27 ms for the mean speaker. Putting this more informally, in modal voice the intervals between 99% of all glottal pulses vary by less than a millisecond. (This is a rough interpretation of the statistics; many qualifications apply.) In creaky-voiced vowels the standard deviation was always greater. It had a range from .58 to 5.07 ms, with a mean of 2.45 ms.

There is a problem in measuring jitter that I have rather brushed over in this discussion so far. Both the creaky-voiced and the modal Jalapa Mazatec vowels were pronounced on a comparatively steady-state fundamental frequency. But if one group of vowels had been pronounced on a level pitch and the other on a falling or rising pitch, the results would have been different. In a vowel with a steady pitch, each glottal pulse interval does not differ appreciably from the mean, but when the pitch is falling or rising the intervals are changing and thus

Table 7.1   The amount of jitter, measured as the standard deviation from the mean in ms, in the modal and creaky vowels of 5 speakers of Jalapa Mazatec.

	Speaker 1	Speaker 2	Speaker 3	Speaker 4	Speaker 5	Mean speaker
Creaky	.62	.58	2.17	5.07	3.81	2.45
Modal	.20	.28	.14	.39	.33	.27

differ from the mean. When measuring jitter you can compensate for overall falling or rising pitch changes by measuring the difference between the observed glottal pulse intervals and those that would have occurred in a smooth fall or rise.

Creaky voice often occurs as the phonetic realization of a phonological glottal stop. Figure 7.5 shows the waveforms of parts of two Montana Salish words, [q'áq'ɬuʔ] 'vein' and [kʷáteʔ] 'quarter' (25 cents,

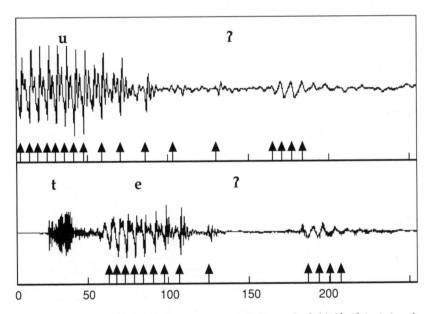

Figure 7.5   The last parts of the Montana Salish words, [q'áq'ɬuʔ] 'vein' and [kʷáteʔ] 'quarter' (25 cents). The arrows below the waveforms are attempts to mark each glottal pulse.

a loan word). This is another case in which it is hard to say exactly when each pulse occurs. I tried to mark the individual pulses in the waveforms in figure 7.5, but it was often unclear what should be counted as a separate glottal pulse. Nevertheless, what is apparent is that the glottal pulses occur at very irregular intervals.

What we really want to know in order to describe different types of phonation is the shape of the glottal pulses produced by the vibrating vocal folds. Usually the vocal folds produce pulses of air as a result of being blown apart and then coming back together again. In modal voice their outward movement is a little slower than the rate at which they come together. Consequently the pulses of air that are produced are asymmetrical, with a slower rise and a sharper descent. Creaky voice and breathy voice produce different pulse shapes. Figure 7.6 shows a

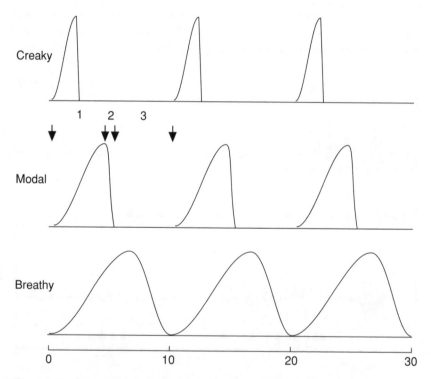

Figure 7.6   Schematized versions of the glottal pulses in three types of phonation. The arrows above the modal pulse mark (1) opening phase, (2) closing phase, (3) closure.

schematized version of the three different phonation types. When producing the creaky voice pulse at the top, the vocal folds come together very rapidly, making the closing phase much shorter than the opening phase. They then remain tightly shut, with a comparatively long closure. In a modal voice the closing phase is shorter than the opening phase, but the two are more nearly the same. In a really breathy voice, as schematized here at the bottom of the figure, the opening and closing phases are much the same length, and there is virtually no closure.

7.2   Spectral Characteristics of Phonation Types

The vocal fold pulses set the air in the vocal tract vibrating in ways that depend on the shapes of the cavities involved. The different shapes produce the formant frequencies that characterize vowels and other sounds. The waveform is a combination of the vocal fold pulse and the resonances associated with the formants. If we want to see the vocal fold pulses, we must find some technique that can disentangle pulses from the rest of the waveform. This can be done by a technique known as inverse filtering, which removes the formant resonances, leaving the vocal fold pulse. It's a complicated technique that works best with comparatively steady-state vowels and high-quality recordings that include even the very low-frequency variations in air pressure, all of which make it difficult to use in most linguistic investigations.

We can, however, infer something about the vocal pulse shape from the spectrograms of a sound. A creaky voice pulse, with a sharp closure, will contribute more to the high frequencies of a sound, and breathy voice vibrations will have much of the energy in the fundamental. Spectrograms of the Newar modal and breathy-voiced nasals discussed earlier are shown in figure 7.7. The modal voice on the left has regular vertical striations corresponding to each opening and closing of the vocal folds, clearly visible in the formants at about 1,500 Hz and 2,000 Hz. In the breathy nasal, the separate pulses are not readily apparent in this region, although they can still be seen in the lower frequencies near the baseline. Because the vocal folds close less sharply in a breathy voice, there is less energy in the higher formants. Much of what energy there is is composed of semi-random noise produced by the turbulent glottal airflow.

The easiest way to measure differences in phonation is by making spectra of the sounds, much as we did in the chapter on vowels. We

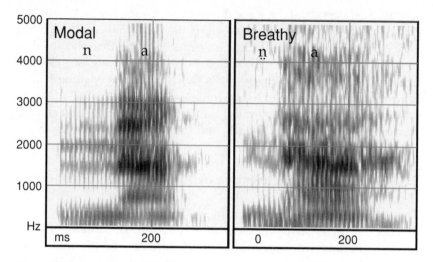

Figure 7.7   Spectrograms of the Newar nasals shown in figure 7.2.

can then measure the relative amount of energy in the higher and lower frequencies. As we have noted, in breathy voice there is relatively more energy in the fundamental frequency (the first harmonic). If we want to assess the amount of breathiness in a sound we need to measure the amount of energy in this frequency in comparison with the rest of the spectrum.

Figure 7.8 shows two ways of doing this for the modal and breathy nasals in figure 7.7. The spectra in this figure were made in the middle of each of the nasals, and arrows have been added showing the intensity level of the first harmonic (H1), the second harmonic (H2), and the harmonic with the highest intensity in the second (nasal) formant, F2. In the nasal with modal voicing (on the left) there is not a great deal of energy in the first harmonic, and H2 is greater than H1. But in the breathy voice nasal on the right there is more energy in the fundamental frequency, and H1 is greater than H2. The second way of measuring the relative amplitude of the first harmonic is to compare it with the amplitude of the harmonic with the highest intensity in the second formant. In both nasals H1 is greater than F2, but the difference (H1 − F2) is far greater in the breathy nasal.

The same kind of calculations can be applied to creaky-voiced sounds. Figure 7.9 shows narrowband spectra of three vowels in San Lucas Quiavíni Zapotec, one of the many Zapotec languages spoken in

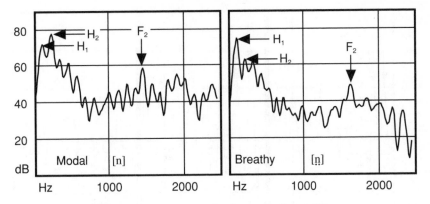

Figure 7.8 Spectra of the Newar nasals shown in figure 7.7.

Mexico. (All the data, figures and graphs of Zapotec in this section are from a study by Matt Gordon.) This language contrasts three phonation types, creaky, modal and breathy.

Perhaps the first point to note in figure 7.9 is that the modal voice (in the middle of the figure) has the overall greatest intensity. Modal voice is the most efficient form of vibration of the vocal folds, and typically has the greatest intensity. But what is more important is the relative intensity of the harmonics in each of these three spectra. As we have noted, in creaky voice the vocal folds snap shut quickly, producing a glottal pulse that has a great deal of energy in the higher frequencies; modal voice produces slightly less energy in these regions; and breathy voice has most energy in the fundamental frequency (the first harmonic).

In the discussion of Newar nasals we compared H1 and H2, and H1 and F2. You can also measure phonation type differences by comparing H1 and F1 or H1 and F3. All these are measures of the slope of the spectrum indicating how much of the energy is in the fundamental frequency as compared with higher frequencies. If F1 has a low frequency, close to that of the fundamental frequency, it is better to use F2. But if F2 differs in the vowels being compared then F1 would be more suitable. If F3 is clearly distinguishable and not too close to a varying F2, then it might be the best candidate. There is no perfect way of measuring the slope of the spectrum that works for all vowels.

A dashed line has been drawn in figure 7.9 at the level of H1 in each of the spectra, making it easier to compare H1 and H2, and H1 and F1.

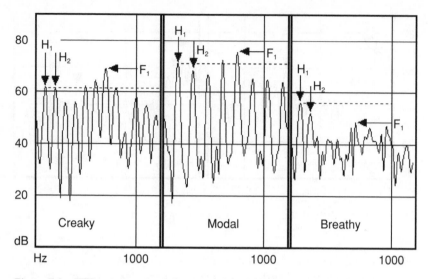

Figure 7.9 FFT spectra of creaky, modal and breathy **a** in San Lucas Quiaviní Zapotec. The dashed line marks the intensity of H1, the first harmonic, in each spectrum.

In creaky voice the second harmonic, H2, has almost the same amplitude as H1. In modal voice H2 is about 2.5 dB lower, and in breathy voice it is a little lower still, about 4 dB below H1. When we compare H1 with the highest harmonic in the first formant, here marked F1, we get similar but not identical results. In creaky voice H1 – F1 = –7.5 dB (the first formant is 7.5 dB above H1). In modal voice the first formant is about 4 dB above H1, and in breathy voice it is nearly 8 dB below H1.

When these relationships are expressed graphically, as in figure 7.10, they can both be seen to reflect a tendency for the downward slope of the spectrum to increase as one moves from creaky through modal to breathy voice. The breathier the voice, the greater the difference between the first harmonic and higher frequencies.

Finally, a note of warning must be sounded over the use of these spectral measures. Differences in phonation are not the only things that can affect the relative intensities of the harmonics. They are also affected by differences in vowel quality; when two formants come close together, their amplitudes are increased. In addition, differences in pitch will affect the amplitudes of the harmonics being measured.

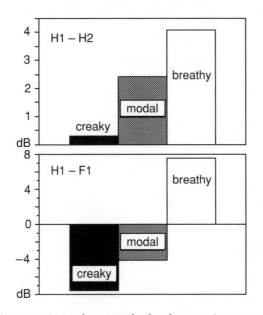

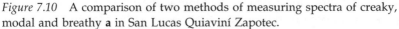

Figure 7.10   A comparison of two methods of measuring spectra of creaky, modal and breathy **a** in San Lucas Quiaviní Zapotec.

Consequently it is important to compare vowels that do not differ in vowel quality or pitch to any great extent. Spectral slope is also affected by stress (a fact pointed out to me by Bert Remisen). Words with a higher stress will have a more positive slope (greater intensities in the higher frequencies), which will interact with measures of phonation type differences.

7.3   Further Reading

Gordon, M. and Ladefoged, P. (2001) Phonation types: a cross-linguistic overview, *Journal of Phonetics*, 29, 383–406.

Ni Chasaide, A. and Gobl, C. (1999) Voice source variation. In Hardcastle, W. J. and Laver, J. (eds.) *The handbook of phonetic sciences*. Oxford: Blackwell (Blackwell Handbooks in Linguistics, 5).

8

Coda

8.1 A General-purpose Phonetics Laboratory

I'm often asked what one needs for a basic general phonetics laboratory. It's a good question to discuss in the concluding chapter of this book, as it provides a way of looking at the preceding chapters and gives me an opportunity to mention a few practical points. I can say what is needed only in general terms, as the world is always changing, and it is impossible to specify exactly which pieces of equipment should be bought. It will be a year after I have written this before the book comes out, and I hope it will stay in print for a while, so if I were to mention a particular model of something, it would be out of date by the time you read about it. But it is possible to list the kinds of things that should be available to people studying speech. Table 8.1 gives the basic requirements. If you need more information, contact me at oldfogey@ucla.edu. I'm always willing to report on whatever new information I have – and if you want help in setting up a phonetics lab in Outer Yucca or some other place, send me a ticket, and I'll be there.

The first essential is a good recording system. We discussed recording techniques in chapter 1, and at that time (more than a year ago for me) I mentioned three possibilities: cassette tapes, DAT tapes and computers. I still stand by them, but I think it is more likely that soon we will all be using some form of digital recording. But whatever the recording medium, we still need to have good microphones, headsets and loudspeakers. Another obvious necessity is a good supply of tape or backup disks.

Table 8.1   Basic instrumentation for phonetic data analysis.

1. Recording system
   Recorder
   Microphone
   Headphones, loudspeaker
   Tape
2. Video camera
   Video tape
3. Palatography
   (Camera)
   Mirrors (at least two)
   Light source
   Charcoal
   Olive oil
   Paintbrushes
   Disinfectant tissues, paper towels
   Dental impression material
   Mixing bowls, spatula, plaster
4. Aerodynamic recording
   Pressure transducers
   Oral flow mask
   Nasal flow mask
   A/D system
   Tubing and connectors
   Syringe
   Disinfectant
5. Electroglottograph
   Electrode jelly or alcohol swabs
6. Computer
   Printer
   Connecting cables
7. Acoustic analysis software

Next in the order discussed in this book were video recorders and palatography. If you don't have a video recorder, then you will need two other items: a spare tape recorder (probably a good idea in any case) and a camera (preferably a digital one) for palatography. I listed all the palatography peripherals, including a light source for illuminating the inside of the mouth. One possibility is a good reading lamp that can be pointed in any direction, but digital cameras are now so

> I've helped start up phonetic analysis systems in a number of countries. On one memorable occasion I arranged for the purchase of a large amount of equipment for a phonetics laboratory – it was almost my dream lab, with all that anyone could need. I did not hear from the professor in charge for almost two years after everything had been bought, when he invited me to visit. I arrived to find that everything was still in its original cartons, gathering dust and damp in a humid boxroom. We were lucky that all of it still worked.

sensitive that even a flashlight will do. Remember that you will need not only some way of disinfecting the palatography mirrors, but also paper towels for cleaning things up. Palatography can be a messy business.

There are incidentals needed with an aerodynamic system, such as the tubes that connect the masks and the flow transducers, and the open-ended tubes that are used for recording pressure. The latter need to be sterile, and it is easiest to buy them as catheters from a medical supply house. Feeding tubes are often an appropriate caliber, though they are much too long. In all aerodynamic recording the tubes should be kept as short as possible, so as to have a good frequency response. Don't forget that you will need a syringe or some way of squirting air through a pressure-recording tube so as to keep it free of mucus. You will also need T-pieces to join the syringe with the tube and the pressure-recording transducer, as shown in figures 3.7 and 3.8.

An electroglottograph is a fairly straightforward instrument requiring few peripherals. Some manufacturers suggest that more reliable contact between the electrodes on either side of the larynx and the neck can be obtained if electrode jelly is applied to the neck. Others suggest that it is sufficient to make sure the neck has been completely cleaned by using an alcohol swab.

The last two items on the list, a computer system and analysis software, are very much a matter of personal taste. It would be inappropriate to add comments here.

Table 8.1 is incomplete from the point of view of anyone wanting to set up a speech analysis system in their institution. It does not mention the need for a quiet place to make recordings. Professionally made soundproofed spaces are the best solution, but they are expensive. If they are not available, look for a quiet room, possibly one that is underground and without a noisy air conditioner and not too close to a roaring furnace room. Heavy doors with rubber seals will help, as will wall hangings and soft furnishings that reduce reverberation. In one lab in my early days we lined the walls with egg-packing cartons.

8.2   More Elaborate Instrumental Phonetic Techniques

This book has been concerned with the basic instrumental phonetic techniques that should be available in a laboratory for the analysis of speech. There are many other ways of investigating articulatory movements and phonation types that are not suitable for use in fieldwork and are not usually available in small phonetics laboratories. We will conclude with some short notes on a few of them, hoping that you might be prompted to see if any of them are available locally. Even in places where there are no provisions for phonetic research there may be hospitals or other laboratories that use these techniques.

The first technique, ultrasound, is rapidly becoming more available, and I would not be surprised at having to include it as a regular fieldwork technique in a future edition of this book. Ultrasound enables one to record the movements of the tongue, including the tongue root, as exemplified in figure 8.1. One can measure the timing of articulatory events (subject to the fact that the frame rate is currently limited to about 30 fps). It is non-invasive and units are now comparatively portable.

Ultrasound images are constructed from the echoes that return when the ultrasound waves pass through soft tissue that changes in density. The biggest echoes are when the soft tissue is bounded by air. As a result, a small transducer held against the neck close to the chin will capture much of the shape of the tongue, as it is bounded by air in the mouth and pharynx. There are problems in that ultrasound will sometimes not show the tip of the tongue when there is air below it as well as above it. But the rest of the tongue can be viewed to produce either the traditional mid-sagittal view, or, by turning the transducer sideways, a side-to-side view of the tongue in a coronal section.

X-rays are generally invasive – harmful to the subject – and are no longer available as a research tool in most US universities. Until suitable systems using low dosage X-rays are available, X-rays should be used only for clinical purposes. The alternative is Magnetic Resonance

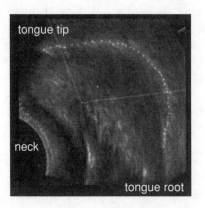

Figure 8.1   An example of an ultrasound scan, showing the tongue in an advanced tongue root vowel in Kinande (adapted from Gick, 2002). The white dots were placed along the tongue edge by an automated edge detection program. A polynomial curve was then fitted through these points. The straight white lines show the main axes of the articulatory movements (root retraction/advancement and body raising/lowering).

Imaging (MRI). This is a technique for viewing articulatory movements, producing a somewhat similar view to that produced by X-rays. MRI is a non-invasive technique (although I must admit that I find it somewhat obnoxious in that one is confined in a small cylinder and subjected to loud banging noises). MRI images show the soft tissue very well, but do not pick out bony structures such as the teeth. Unlike X-rays they can show a particular plane, e.g. the mid-sagittal section, as in figure 8.2.

Static MRI images can provide considerable detail, but cine MRI has less definition. A short movie of the Belgian phonetician Didier Demolin producing the five vowels **i, e, a, o, u** can be found on the CD accompanying my book, *Vowels and consonants* (Blackwell 2001), or on the web at: http://hctv.humnet.ucla.edu/departments/linguistics/ VowelsandConsonants/vowels/chapter11/tongue.html. (Like many movie clips, this file may take some time to download.) At the moment MRI movies can be made only at limited frame rates. The movie cited above was made at five frames per second, resulting in rather jerky movements, and 10 frames per second is the top rate for many systems. (By the time this book comes out it may be possible to use higher frame rates.) MRI systems are expensive, and rarely found outside

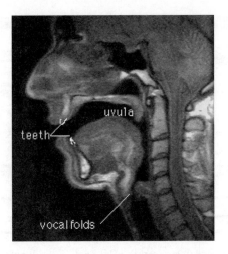

Figure 8.2   An MRI view of the head. The front teeth have been outlined in white. (From Ladefoged 2001.)

hospitals. But you can sometimes find a hospital that will donate access time for research purposes.

An imaging technique that is available in some phonetics labs is the Electromagnetic (Midsagittal) Articulography (EMA or EMMA) system. In this technique small sensors are placed on the articulators (typically the tongue and lips, with additional reference sensors on fixed points such as the chin and the nose). A set of magnetic field generators around the head produces high-frequency magnetic fields. Each of these fields induces a voltage that is proportional to the distance between the sensors and the particular generator producing that field. Depending on the system, EMA allows the movements of 5 to 28 points to be recorded. An adhesive has to be used to keep the sensors in place, so it is difficult to get them on less accessible parts of the vocal tract, such as the pharynx and the root of the tongue.

EMA is more limited than ultrasound or MRI as it shows the locations of a set of points on the lips and tongue, rather than the articulators as a whole. However, EMA has a major advantage in that it provides a virtually continuous record of the movements of these points. The locations of the sensors are recorded 500 times per second, which is high enough to capture all the details of articulatory movements. Furthermore, EMA provides not only more detail about the points

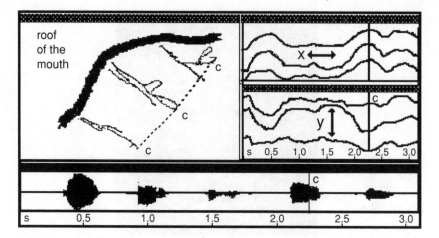

Figure 8.3   Movement data from the Carsten's articulograph. The left-hand window shows the movements of three points on the tongue, the right-hand window the x–y locations of each of the points, and the lower window the waveform of the phrase, **a, e, i, o, u**. The dashed line in the left-hand window joins the locations of the three sensors at the time of the cursors in the left-hand window and waveform, marked **c**. The labels and time scales have been added to the original display

being recorded, but also more readily available numerical data than X-rays or MRI. Older X-ray movies are typically at 25 frames per second, and MRI is currently limited to 10 fps. Having to make measurements on each frame is a tedious process, even with a good analysis system such as NIH Image (freely downloadable from http://rsb.info.nih.gov/nih-image). It is much better to have virually continuous records already in numerical form on a computer.

Typical EMA records (from the Carstens Articulograph) are shown in figure 8.3. The thick line in the left-hand panel shows the position of the roof of the mouth, obtained by moving the sensors along the midline from the teeth to the soft palate. There were three sensors on the tongue, one on the blade near the tip and two others further back. The speaker said the vowel sequence **a, e, i, o, u**, with the waveform being shown in the lower panel. The right-hand panel shows, in the upper part, the x (horizontal) positions, and, in the lower part, the y (vertical) positions of each sensor at each moment in time (the time scale has been added to this panel and to the waveform panel). These locations have been plotted in the left-hand panel, which does not have a time scale as it shows the sensor locations throughout the utterance. The cursor is placed in the middle of the o on the wave-form, with its position being reflected in the x–y locations in the right-hand panel. A dashed line in the left-hand panel joins the three sensor locations at this time. The tongue is in a mid-high back position for this vowel (remember that tongue positions often differ from their supposed positions).

The Carstens Articulograph can also provide dynamic records and other graphs, such as the velocity at which each sensor is moving at each moment in time, so that you can see when the tongue is moving most rapidly.

A number of techniques for investigating phonation types and pharyngeal movement may be available in the laryngology depart-ment of your local hospital. There will probably be a way to photo-graph the vocal folds using a laryngoscope, but often this involves a rigid rod and lens system, making it impossible to talk. You can get good photographs of the vibrating vocal folds in a vowel (mine are shown at http://hctv.humnet.ucla.edu/departments/linguistics/VowelsandConsonants/vowels/chapter2/vibrating%20cords/vibrating.html), but the rigid rod prevents you from talking normally. If you are fortunate there may be a system for fiberoptic laryngoscopy, a system using a flexible tube containing a grid of fiberoptic fibers. With only moderate difficulty this tube can be passed through the nose, causing no interference with most sentences. The lens on one end of the fiberoptic bundle can be positioned a few centimeters above the vocal folds and the other end connected to a camera. This system can capture good pictures of the vibrating vocal folds in regular utterances. It can also be used to view movements of the root of the tongue and the epiglottis such as those that occur in pharyngeal sounds. Figure 8.4 shows the state of the glottis during initial **h** in English.

8.3   Before and After Fieldwork

I use something like table 8.1 as a checklist before I go out into field, but in this respect it is incomplete in that it does not stress the necessity of backup. Ideally one wants two of everything, certainly of small things like flashlights, and even if possible of major things like computers. On our last trip in the Kalahari Desert we accidentally

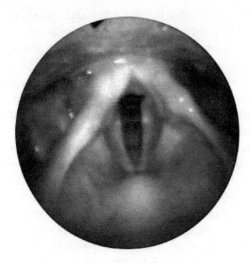

Figure 8.4   An example of fiberoptic laryngoscopy data, courtesy of John Esling, Phonetics Laboratory, Department of Linguistics, University of Victoria, B.C.

poured a jug of water over my laptop computer. Fortunately my wife had hers with her, so all was not lost. There are some other small items that you should remember, as things always go wrong, and you need to be able to deal with them. In addition to some multipurpose tool or Swiss army knife, I have a supply of chewing gum (very useful for holding two wires together, as I found when repairing part of the ignition system that had caught fire), modeling clay (holds mirrors in place when photographing side views of the face), and duct tape (straps things together when the screws have fallen out).

Another lack in table 8.1 is that it doesn't mention something else that should be checked before going out into the field – health precautions. Be sure that you have all your inoculations, and, if you are going into malarial regions, that you have started your anti-malarial drugs. I take basic medical supplies such as a simple anti-bacterial ointment, aspirin and a diarrhea preventative. I'm also a great believer in some anti-itch ointment for insect bites of all kinds.

If you take simple safety measures, fieldwork should create no health problems. On one occasion when I was at the University of Port Harcourt, Nigeria, power and water were available for only two hours each morning. All the students at the university had been sent home

Very occasionally there are some serious hazards in doing fieldwork. The only time I felt in real danger was in Nigeria, when I landed at Lagos airport late at night. I took a taxicab around the perimeter of the airport to the domestic terminal, where I was due to catch a small plane in the morning. As we were driving along a deserted stretch of road a big Mercedes roared alongside us and forced my taxi to stop. A couple of men jumped out and yelled, 'Come, sir, come with us in our car.' I sat still while they continued, 'Come with us sir, the boss sent us to pick you and we missed you at the airport.' When I didn't move they yelled some more: 'Get out of your taxi, sir, the chief says you must come with us.' I asked, 'Who is the chief?' and got the reply, 'The boss, sir, get out and come with us.' I asked if they knew my name. 'Of course, sir, get out now, and bring your passport. Your name is on your passport.' I was lucky that by then my driver had worked out what was happening. He indicated that he thought he could get round the other car, and thankfully I told him to drive on as fast as he could.

because of health risks. I bought a bucket and an immersion heater intended for a hot water cistern (Port Harcourt is a large busy city where you can buy almost anything – when the stores are open). I boiled a bucket of water every morning, and made a gallon of very weak tea that I could drink steadily through the day. You can get very dehydrated in Nigeria if you just sit and sweat; and you should never drink unboiled water. Fortunately, through following a few simple precautions like not eating uncooked vegetables or unpeeled fruit, I've never been sick while doing fieldwork. It's often been polite to join in eating unusual food. I've eaten fried termites (a little crisp, but quite tasty), braided goat's intestines (prepared by Jenny, my wife, after having been shown by a Yoruba woman how to turn them inside out and braid them), and many kinds of animal from lion and giraffe to gazelle. None of them made me ill, as they had all been properly cooked.

At the very end of the book it is time for me to remind you of the concluding steps of any set of experiments or fieldwork investigation. It's nice to end with a party, saying goodbye to all who have helped. It is also the time to wind up loose ends in people's expectations, which probably involve a parting present or actual payment. Apart from really helpful things, like giving the group a cow or making a donation to a local cultural center, small gifts such as photographs are often

It is always important to get the support of the local community so that you can get what help you need. This often involves sitting around doing nothing for some time. As far as I can find out, my son Thegn, who is an archeologist, spent much of his first few weeks on a small island in the Pacific hanging out with his age group, drinking kava, a narcotic brew made from a local plant. As a father I am not sure about the drinking part, but it paid off in that he became well regarded. After a couple of weeks, one of the elders came up to him and said, 'Come along son, it's now time to show you where the old people lived.' And he went to work.

much appreciated. If there is a local university or cultural center they would probably appreciate a talk about what you are doing.

Of course the end of data gathering is not the beginning of analysis. That should have begun long ago. Whatever kind of experiment or fieldwork you have been conducting, you should have been analyzing your data as you go. Now is the time to consolidate it all and finish writing it up. My aim, seldom achieved but always attempted, is to write the introduction to a paper, laying out the background and stating the problem, before doing anything else. I also try to write up the procedure section before beginning, so that I know what I will be doing. Procedures get modified as one goes along, so this section has to be rewritten; but again this should be done while collecting the data, not after it has all been collected. You should even try to write up the results section of the paper as you go along, just leaving a few blanks for the actual numbers. That way, when you leave the lab or the field site, all that you have to do is the final consolidation of the results you have been getting.

After you have written everything, I hope you will publish a complete account of the work, even if is only on your own web site. Private knowledge does the world no good. After all, I hope it won't happen, but you might be run over by a bus tomorrow, and then all your work will be lost. In addition, make sure that your data is stored in such a way that it can be found and used by others. Even if no one else wants to look at it, you yourself may want to go back to it in future years (assuming the bus missed you), and without it being properly stored as interpretable records, you may have forgotten exactly what you did. Lastly, make sure that your language consultants or speakers know how it all turned out. Send them a copy of the report.

This is not just a matter of being polite, although it is also that. It ensures that investigators who come after you will get a good reception. We want people to know that finding out about languages is fun. We enjoy doing it, so let's make sure that others share in our delight.

8.4   Further Reading

Esling, John H. (1999). The IPA categories 'pharyngeal' and 'epiglottal': Laryngoscopic observations of pharyngeal articulations and larynx height. *Language & Speech*, 42, 349–72.

Esling, John H., and Edmondson, Jerold A. (2002). The laryngeal sphincter as an articulator: Tenseness, tongue root and phonation in Yi and Bai. In Angelika Braun and Herbert R. Masthoff (eds.), *Phonetics and its applications: Festschrift for Jens-Peter Köster on the occasion of his 60th birthday*, pp. 38–51. Stuttgart: Franz Steiner Verlag.

Gick, B. (2002). The use of ultrasound for linguistic phonetic fieldwork. *Journal of the International Phonetic Association*, 32.2.

Ladefoged, P. (2001) *Vowels and consonants*. Oxford: Blackwell.

Narayanan, S., D. Byrd, and Kaun, A. (1999). Geometry, kinematics, and acoustics of Tamil liquid consonants. *Journal of the Acoustical Society of America*, 1993–2007.

Index